EDUCATIONAL
MEASUREMENT
AND
EVALUATION

EDUCATIONAL MEASUREMENT AND EVALUATION

DON F. BLOOD

WILLIAM C. BUDD

Western Washington State College

HARPER AND ROW, Publishers
New York, Evanston, San Francisco, London

Standard Book Number: 06–041029–9
Library of Congress Catalog Card Number: 70–178108

CONTENTS

PREFACE

Whether he relishes the role or not, a teacher is, of necessity, an evaluator. As a facilitator of learning, it is his duty to inform students of how well they are doing in order to provide them with the feedback so necessary to their intellectual and academic development. Since he cannot escape this duty, it is to his own advantage to perform it as ably as he can. The basic purpose of this book is to aid teachers in the skillful execution of this vital professional function.

In teaching, educational evaluation is closely associated with educational measurement. Judgments of student progress made by teachers should be based, insofar as possible, on the best available evidence. Such evidence typically comes not from unstructured observations, but from some form of measurement. It is a basic premise of this book that educational evaluation can best be improved by improving educational measurement.

This book is addressed to professional teachers, both those in practice and those in training. The examples used to illustrate concepts and principles are taken from the classroom. The major emphasis of the book is upon the preparation of teacher-made tests, although one chapter is devoted to a brief discussion of standardized tests. The treatment of the basic content of educational measurement is succinct, yet easily understandable.

This is not a theoretical book on educational measurement. The principles and procedures recommended are based not so much on research as on practical experience. It is the contention of the authors that the production of good measuring instruments in education is more of an art than a science.

Theory does intrude into the book, however, in two places: (1) a discussion of the basic nature of educational measurement, and (2) an explanation of the concept of validity. With respect to the first, the authors argue that educational measurement need not be bound by the strictures of mathematics. With respect to the second, the authors argue for the concept of "relevance" as a basic component of validity.

The book is sufficiently short that it can be used either as a basic text or as a supplementary text in courses devoted in whole or in part to the problems of educational measurement and evaluation. Since the orientation of the book is principally toward measures of relative achievement, instructors may wish to supplement it with materials more specifically devoted to mastery testing. As a basic text, it could also be used in conjunction with books of readings.

The authors owe a special debt of gratitude to Dr. Merle E. Meyer, Chairman of the Department of Psychology at Western Washington State College, for his encouragement and support in the writing and preparation of the manuscript for this book.

DON F. BLOOD
WILLIAM C. BUDD

EDUCATIONAL
MEASUREMENT
AND
EVALUATION

1
THE NATURE OF EDUCATIONAL MEASUREMENT

The ability to use and understand certain kinds of measurement is part of the professional responsibility of the teacher. In this respect, teaching is no different from other professions that also include measurement as a part of their standard practice. We cannot readily conceive, for example, of a physician who knows neither how to measure blood pressure nor how to interpret the measures which he obtains, nor can we readily conceive of a mechanical engineer who does not know how to measure stresses. Yet we are frequently quite willing to accept the subjective impressions of teachers concerning student achievement in place of more precise measures, because we still like to feel that teaching is more of an art than a science. This it may be, but no one has yet demonstrated that increased precision is detrimental even to an art. The education of teachers should not neglect those areas of practice where some element of precision is possible. Educational measurement is one such area. No teacher should be considered professionally competent who does not know at least the rudiments of the theory and practice of educational measurement. This book is an attempt to provide instruction in those rudiments.

First we must begin by defining what we mean by *measurement*. Producing a satisfactory definition of measurement is not so easy a task as it might at first seem. Let us begin with a standard dictionary definition. Measurement is the "act or process of ascertaining the extent, dimensions, quantity, etc. of something, especially by comparison with a standard."[1] This is certainly the type of definition which would be acceptable to most persons. There is, however, at least one technical criticism which could be made of it. This criticism concerns the use of the word "something." The word carries an unfortunate materialistic connotation which the lexicographers may or may not have intended. Let us illustrate what we mean. What is the "something" which is measured when we measure intelligence? Or aptitude? Or achievement? Intelligence, aptitude and achievement are all abstract words referring to supposed mental processes. Such processes may or may not have any empirical reality. In the language of the scientist, they are called *constructs*. We have learned long ago, at our intellectual peril, to avoid reifying such constructs. Yet the tendency to think that we are, in fact, still measuring "something" tends to persist.

A more fruitful way of defining what we actually mean by "measurement" might be to approach the problem by way of the concept of the variable. A *variable* is simply the name given to any descriptive notion applied to things (persons, objects, events, or even ideas) where such things may fall at different points from high to low along a scale designed to apply to this notion. For example, take the notion of height. Height is a variable because different objects can assume different points

---

[1] *The Random House Dictionary of the English Language* (unabridged edition), edited by Jess Stein (Random House, New York, 1966), p. 888.

on a scale said to provide "measures" of height. If all possible objects fell at the same scale point, the notion of height would have no descriptive value. It would not be a variable.

Now things can vary in one of two basic ways: continuously or discontinuously (also called discretely). A continuous variable is one where the things described by this variable may assume any possible point on the scale. For a discontinuous variable on the other hand, the things described must necessarily be found at only specific points along the scale. In continuous variation, the unit that is used to describe the variation can logically be infinitely subdivided into smaller subunits. In discontinuous variation, the unit cannot be subdivided without doing logical damage to its meaning. In continuous variation, the numbers that are attached to things according to their position along the scale are obtained by measurement. In discontinuous variation, such numbers are obtained by enumeration.

Let us attempt to clarify the difference between continuous and discontinuous variation through the use of examples. Height is an example of a continuous variable. Note that if we use one of our usual systems for assessing height, say a yardstick, it is theoretically possible for things to be placed at any point on such a scale. One thing might be placed at the point 2 ft. 3 1/2 in. Another might be placed at the point 2 ft. 3.34 in., or even 2 ft. 3.3338 in. It is also readily apparent that the unit here employed to describe height, the inch, is capable of infinite subdivision. We may subdivide the inch so far as expedience demands. Class size, on the other hand, is an example of a discontinuous variable. The unit that is used to describe class size is the individual student. We say that one class contains 29 students; another contains 30 students. No class even contains 29 1/2 students. It is not possible for a class to fall at any point along this scale except at those points labeled by whole numbers. Nor can we subdivide the unit in any meaningful fashion. Note also that the numbers used to describe the size of classes are obtained by a process of enumeration or counting. We would not apply the term "measurement" to such a process.

Measurement, then, is a term which is restricted in application to continuous variables. Since that is the case, let us attempt another definition of measurement. Let us say that measurement is the use of any systematic process for quantifying a continuous variable. Then let us follow the implications of such a definition. First of all, note the use of the word "systematic." This simply means that the procedures employed must be made sufficiently explicit and regular so that anyone with the necessary background and training can employ them. This would exclude any largely intuitive means for assessing variables. The person claiming discovery of a new measuring process must be able to say what the procedures are and must be able to train other persons to use them.

Next, quantification of a variable means that in relation to this variable, and as a basic minimum, it must be possible for us to say of three things, A, B, and C, that $A > B$ and $B > C$; therefore, $A > C$. If we cannot say this, we have not been able to establish quantitative differences among the things, and thus we have been unable to measure them.

Now one might object that this definition allows for all sorts of quackery in the name of measurement. For example, someone could assert that he measures intelligence by ascertaining the amount of light reflected at a precisely determined spot on a child's forehead. The procedure would be systematic, and the inventor could train others to do it. He could also assert that children differ systematically and quantitatively on his measures. It would, in fact, qualify as a measurement process. Fortunately, our innovator would also be forced to convince others of the worth of his procedures and demonstrate a useful relation between his measures and measures on other variables already available on these children. Unless he could demonstrate, for example, that his measures predict school achievement better than the results of currently available intelligence tests, his "test" would likely be rather shabbily received. Moreover, in light of the procedures employed, the test would undoubtedly be accused of cultural bias.

For some years now, in discussing measurement theory, it has been standard practice to place all types of measurements into one of four measurement *scales* called the nominal, ordinal, interval, and ratio scales. The *nominal* scale is characterized by numbers that bear no hierarchical relation to each other but are used simply as labels to designate different kinds or classes of things. We could, for example, when punching IBM cards, use the digit 0 to stand for females and the digit 1 to stand for males. This practice would be in good keeping with the precepts of Freudian psychoanalytic psychology. The *ordinal* scale is characterized by a hierarchical relation among numbers. Here we could, for example, designate the winners of a beauty contest by the numbers 1, 2, and 3. As is the usual order of things in such contests, we can say with relation to the attribute in question that $1 > 2$, $2 > 3$; therefore, $1 > 3$. We cannot say, however, by how much 1 differs from 2 or 2 from 3. Nor do we typically have a zero point on such a scale. There would be nothing to prevent us from assigning the number 0 to the winner of a beauty contest, but since 0 has the connotation of a starting place or perhaps the absence of an attribute, it would be emotionally difficult for us to accept this usage. The interval scale is characterized by the presence of a logical (though arbitrary) zero point and equal units along the scale. The centigrade scale for measuring temperature is usually cited as an example of an interval scale. The *ratio* scale is like the interval scale in possessing equal units. It differs in that its zero point is a "true" zero rather than an arbitrary zero. True zero means complete absence of the variable being measured. Measures of height, for example, exemplify a ratio scale.

Now the importance of this fourfold classification scheme is said to be that the type of mathematical treatment which can be given to the numbers representing measures depends upon the particular scale to which such measures belong. The numbers belonging to a nominal scale can be afforded only very limited mathematical treatment. No rational person would attempt to predict the outcome of a football game by adding the numbers on the backs of the starting teams and picking the team with the larger sum as the potential victor. About all we can do with such numbers is to report the frequency with which they occur. In the case of our IBM cards, we could report the relative frequencies of 0's and 1's in our entering freshman class. We can do more things with numbers representing ordinal scales. We can, for example, convert such numbers into percentile rankings; we can calculate the median of such numbers, and we can employ many of the so-called "nonparametric" tests to distinguish possible differences between groups described by such ordinal numbers. Numbers from interval scales are open to all types of mathematical treatment save one. This is the matter of ratios, which belongs only to those numbers from a ratio scale. We cannot legitimately say, for example, that 40°C is twice as hot as 20°C. We can say, however, that 40 in. is twice 20 in.

There are certain difficulties with this fourfold classification scheme. In the first place, the nominal scale does not fit our definition of measurement. Nor does it fit the dictionary definition, or the definition held implicitly by the man in the street. The typical citizen would not consider differentiating between boys and girls, no matter how difficult the task might become, a matter of measurement. The fact that numbers are assigned to the outcome makes no difference to him. He is not so easily fooled. He might call the process classification, or differentiation, or (if a true activist) discrimination, but he would not call it measurement. He implicitly recognizes that measurement pertains only to a single continuous variable. Sex, so we have been told, is a dichotomous variable.

The second difficulty with this scheme is that for years it has placed the scores from educational and psychological tests in a sort of mathematical limbo. The basic question always raised is the question of the scale to which such test scores belong. The choice narrows down to two scales, ordinal or interval. Those who argue for the higher scale will point out that the numbers derived from an achievement test do have a zero point, albeit an arbitrary one determined by the test itself. Moreover, they will argue, the unit employed has a clear unequivocal meaning which is constant along the length of the scale. The number

55, for example, means one more item answered correctly than the number of correct answers represented by the number 54. Similarly, 56 means one more item answered correctly than the total represented by the number 55. At this point, the critic will point out that this apparent uniformity of meaning of the unit employed is illusory. The number 55 does not represent the same 54 items answered correctly plus one more. It represents, instead, a different combination of items altogether. It is only that the outcome of the one combination represents a sum one point higher than the sum of the other combination. Moreover, the items are typically not equal in difficulty. To answer a certain item correctly obviously demands more of the ability or achievement being measured than answering another, easier item. For these and similar reasons, the critics conclude, educational test scores can only be considered to belong to an ordinal scale.

This conclusion is painful to the expert in educational measurement. If he accepts it, it means that he must refrain from carrying out many of his favorite mathematical treatments of test scores. The worst of all restrictions is that he cannot calculate means and standard deviations. This he cannot abide. He insists that no one can tell him not to do what he has been doing for years, and continues to compute means and standard deviations as if he had never heard of the difference between ordinal and interval scales.

The most reasonable position to take is that it is perfectly legitimate for him to make such calculations. This situation, and the doubt it engenders, is another good example of the fact that we frequently mistake mathematical truth for empirical truth. By now we should realize that it is only a happy coincidence when the world of mathematics fits the world of empirical reality. Even when the two worlds overlap, the edges are not smooth. In this case, educational test scores do not fit neatly into either of the two rubrics in question. They do not clearly belong to an interval scale; neither do they clearly belong to an ordinal scale. We cannot legitimately claim that this is the fault of the test scores. It is more appropriately the fault of the classification scheme.

It seems obvious that this scheme was designed to apply to measurements typical of those in the natural sciences, where the variables being measured possessed reasonably unitary meaning. Length, weight, velocity, and pressure are clearly more unitary concepts than intelligence, aptitude, and achievement. One can even question whether it is legitimate to speak of a single variable called achievement, or whether this is not, in fact, just a convenient way of dealing simultaneously with a host of more unitary variables that it would be difficult to deal with singularly.

This book is concerned with the measurement of educational achievement. We shall consider educational achievement to be a continuous variable amenable to measurement. We shall consider the measures so obtained to represent either an ordinal scale or an interval scale, depending upon the procedures employed in obtaining them. If the measures are derived from observational tests, they will normally be considered ordinal in nature. If they are derived from paper and pencil tests, the measures will be considered interval. Mathematical treatments appropriate for both scales will be described.

2
VALIDITY: RELIABILITY AND RELEVANCE

The most important characteristic of any measuring instrument is its validity. *Validity* may be defined as the consistency with which an instrument measures the variable or variables it was designed to measure. Note that this definition may be divided into two parts. The first part concerns the consistency of measurement. This defines that aspect of validity we call *reliability*. The second part concerns the extent to which an instrument measures the variable or variables it was designed to measure. This defines that aspect of validity we call *relevance*. Both must be present to some extent if the instrument is to possess any validity. If one or the other is absent, there can be no validity. The problems of estimating the validity of any measuring instrument, such as a classroom achievement test, are the problems of estimating reliability and relevance.

9

ESTIMATING RELIABILITY

In order for a test to be said to be measuring anything at all, it must measure "something" consistently. If it does not measure something consistently, there is no way of determining what it does measure. In technical terms, we would say that there was no systematic component to the variance of the test scores, and all of the variance must be attributed to various sources of error. If this occurs, the scores possess neither reliability nor validity. This, obviously, seldom if ever occurs in actual practice.

Normally, we can assume that a classroom test will possess some measure of reliability. In other words, it will measure the achievement of students with some degree of *consistency*. What do we mean by "consistency" of measurement?

Let us first illustrate this idea with an example of the measurement of a physical object. Suppose we take a small stick, say one somewhere in the neighborhood of 6 in. long. And suppose we take a typical ruler 1 ft. long and ask 100 college students to use the ruler to measure the stick. Each student measures the stick independently, that is, without knowledge of the results obtained by the other 99. Each student writes his estimate of the length of the stick on a piece of paper, so that at the end of our little demonstration we have 100 pieces of paper each containing an estimate of the length of the stick. An appropriate question at this point would be: Would all 100 estimates be the same? The answer obviously is: No. If we ask why the estimates are not all the same, we could come up with a variety of possible explanations. We might say, for example, that despite some 12 or more years of experience in using a simple device like a ruler, people still differ in their ability to use it accurately. Or there might be motivational factors. Some people took the job seriously and took care to be accurate; others hurried through the task and put down whatever answer seemed reasonable. Perhaps physical factors had something to do with the estimates—the surface where stick and ruler were laid, or the amount and direction of the light falling on the two objects. There would likely be a host of other factors which might account in part for the variability observed in the estimates, but those just cited will do as examples.

Next we might ask the seemingly innocuous question: Does any of the 100 estimates we received equal the *true length* of the stick? Does it not seem intuitively apparent that the stick must, in fact, possess a true length, and that likely one or more of our 100 estimates would coincide with this true length? This seems intuitively true, and so our next question would be: Which one? Now we are stopped, because we find it impossible to say which of the estimates reported equals the true length of the stick. At this point, the statistician proposes a solution. He says that since we can agree that no one really knows the true length of the stick, why do we not select one of the estimates and arbitrarily call this its true length. Let us select this estimate in such a way that we shall minimize the possibility of error. We can minimize the possibility of error by selecting an estimate from the middle of the group of estimates. The statistician might add, speaking somewhat technically, that the mean estimate would be best because it is most reliable. Since we have no better solution to propose, we are likely to accept his advice and counsel.

But let us examine the implications of his solution to this problem. We could begin by arranging all 100 estimates in the form of a frequency distribution. It might conceivably look like this (Fig. 2.1) if

Figure 2.1 Distribution of estimates of length of stick.

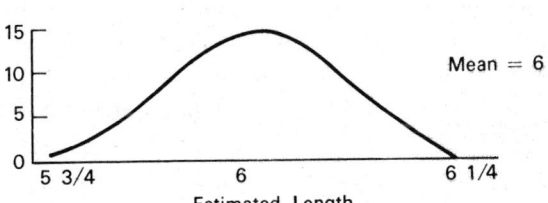

our lowest estimate was 5 3/4 in., our highest estimate was 6 1/4 in., and our mean estimate was 6 in.

Since we have agreed to let the mean estimate be our best estimate of the true length of the stick, we arbitrarily say that the true length of the stick is 6 in. From this statement, it follows that any estimate other than 6 in. is in error to the extent that it differs from 6 in. For example, anyone who estimated the length to be 5 7/8 in. is wrong by 1/8 in. Similarly, anyone who estimated 6 3/32 in. is wrong by 3/32 in. Since this is the case, what our distribution really represents is a distribution of error. Had there been no error, all of the estimates would have fallen at 6 in., and there would be no frequency distribution. Since there is a frequency distribution, and since this distribution results from the fact that all estimates other than 6 in. are in error, the distribution is, in fact, a distribution of such error. At this point, the statistician would point out that we need some way to describe or report the magnitude of the error we observe in this distribution, and he would likely suggest the standard deviation as an appropriate measure. He would call a standard deviation calculated from such a distribution by a special name. He would call it a *standard error of measurement*. Like other standard deviations, the standard error of measurement is an index of the variability of the measures from which it was calculated. In this case, it is an index of the variability of the errors of measurement in this particular demonstration.

Now the standard error of measurement is one way of estimating the reliability of a set of measures. If the standard error is small, it means that the measures are tightly clustered about their central tendency, and any one of the measures taken at random would give a good estimate of the "true" measure you are attempting to estimate. If the standard error is large, on the other hand, the error is rather widely distributed, and any single measure chosen at random might give us a rather error-laden estimate of the true measure. In the first instance, the measures are consistent with each other and we can place high confidence in any one of them as a reasonable estimate of true measure.

In the latter case, the measures are not consistent. They disagree among themselves, and we would not be willing to place much confidence in any one of them as an estimate of the true measure.

Let us see if we could apply the same kind of reasoning to the measurement of another variable—in this case, academic achievement. For purposes of illustration, let us assume that we wish to obtain a large number of independent measures of a given student's achievement in the area of basic arithmetic processes. Each measure would be the outcome of a test which he takes for purposes of the demonstration. Such a situation would demand that we have a large number of *equivalent forms* of the test. We can define equivalent forms rather roughly as two or more forms having about the same length or number of items, having the same difficulty, variability, and reliability, and representing random samples from the same universe of items. If we had, say, 100 equivalent forms of our basic arithmetic test, we could give them on successive days to our student who had volunteered for the demonstration. As in the case of the stick, not all 100 test scores would agree with each other. We would get a distribution of scores clustering around some central value. We could arbitrarily call the mean of this distribution the *true score* for our student. This, in effect, is one way the statistician defines the concept of true score, except that he increases to infinity the number of equivalent forms necessary to identify the true score. Any score which differs from this true score contains a measure of error, and the distribution of observed scores can be considered a distribution of error. The standard deviation of this distribution could be calculated and called the standard error of measurement.

But there is one big difference between the measurement of a variable such as length and the measurement of a variable such as academic achievement. The difference is that, in the first case, we can assume that the variable is not influenced by the act of measurement. Our stick is not changed in length because 100 people have measured it. We cannot legitimately make that assumption in that case of academic achievement. Consider, for example, how much more proficient our hypothetical student would be in arithmetic after taking the ninetieth test, or the fiftieth, or even the tenth. Students learn from even a single administration of a test, and so the variable measured cannot be considered to be entirely unchanged.

This means that we have to seek some other way of estimating the reliability of an achievement test which will reduce to a reasonable minimum the number of times a given student is tested. We intuitively recognize that reducing to a minimum the number of measures on a student will also reduce the reliability of those measures. How can we compensate for this? We compensate by increasing the number of students on whom we have a minimum number of measures. Rather than working with one student, we shall work with 20, or 100, or 1000. The more, the better, within the realm of practicality.

We shall also need some new way of expressing reliability, because now, instead of 100 measures on one individual, we have, say, two measures on each of 100 individuals. What can we use for an index? Fortunately, the coefficient of correlation in its manifold forms is admirably suited to data presented in this fashion, that is, two observations on each of N individuals. Thus, the typical procedure for estimating the reliability of a test becomes some method of obtaining two scores on that test for each student, correlating these scores, and calling the result the coefficient of reliability or the *reliability coefficient*.

The next question is: How do you obtain two scores on a test for each of N students? Typically, three answers have been given to this question:

1. Test and then retest with the same form.
2. Use two equivalent forms of the test.
3. Derive two scores from a single administration of a test.

Each of these three procedures possesses advantages and disadvantages.

The first of these approaches seems most logical and straightforward. If, by reliability, we mean the consistency with which a test measures, then if we give a test once to a group of individuals, and then test them later with the same test, the results ought to be fairly stable. That is, the individuals who scored high the first time ought to score high the second time. Those who scored low should score low on both occasions. We would be suspicious if low-scoring individuals went to the top of the distribution upon retesting. We would logically say that the results were not very reliable; that is, neither the score from the initial or second test could be taken as a good indication of the person's true score on the variable being measured.

Unfortunately, although logic recommends the test-retest procedure for estimating reliability, certain practical considerations militate against its use. First of all, there are seldom many educational situations where it seems appropriate to give a test twice, unless you are attempting to obtain gain scores. Since gain scores are less reliable than test scores, there is seldom much justification for this procedure. A more serious drawback, however, is the change in the variable being measured and other detrimental influences of the initial test. Changes will occur between the first and second testing. Some of these may be because of learning which derives from the test. Since the second test contains exactly the same sample as the first, you are not getting an independent measure of achievement at the time of the second testing. Moreover, the answers which students give the second time are strongly affected by the answers they gave the first time. Where students know the answer, they will obviously respond in the same way. But even when they are not sure of the answer, they will tend to respond the same way they did the first time. This will result in a spuriously high reliability coefficient which would not have occurred had independent samples of items been employed. Because of these objections, the test-retest approach to estimating the reliability of a classroom achievement is seldom, if ever, employed.

The *equivalent forms* approach to estimating test reliability is the one employed by most professional test publishers. It is also the approach which provides the basis for most theoretical interpretations and explanations of the meaning of reliability found in the professional journals devoted to measurement theory. The requirements for this approach are seemingly simple. All you need are two equivalent forms of a test which you administer to the same group of individuals. You calculate a coefficient of reliability from the two scores so derived. The assumption underlying this procedure is that the two forms are essentially random samples from the same universe of items, and thus give independent estimates of the true scores of each individual. If the test is reliable, these two scores should differ only because of random error resulting from the sampling of items plus other miscellaneous sources of error connected with the testing procedures, testing situation, and persons tested.

From the classroom teacher's point of view, however, this apparent simplicity is deceptive. It is not easy to produce equivalent forms of a test. Moreover, in the typical classroom procedure, there is seldom any need to do so. Normally, we produce only one form of a test. What we must do then, is find some way of estimating reliability from the use of a single test form which does not involve using it in retesting.

The so-called *split-halves* or *split-test* procedure is the one which is most practical from the point of view of the classroom teacher. In this procedure, we derive two independent estimates by splitting the test in half for scoring purposes. Although a number of methods can be employed for assigning items to part scores, by far the most common approach is to obtain one part score by scoring the odd-numbered items and another part score by scoring the even-numbered items. Thus we have two scores for each of our students and can use these scores to calculate a coefficient of correlation. The assumption underlying the split-halves procedure is that the two subscores are roughly analogous to the two scores which would be derived from a pair of equivalent forms of the test. They differ only in one significant way: They are based upon tests which are now only half as long as the original test. Since reliability is to some extent a function of the length of a test, a coefficient of correlation calculated using such subscores will give a spuriously low estimate of the true reliability of the test. To correct for this underestimate, the resulting correlation coefficient is normally artificially increased in magnitude using the so-called Spearman-Brown formula. For use in a split-test procedure, this formula is given as

$$r_1 = \frac{2r_s}{r_s + 1},$$ (2.1)

where r_1 is the estimated true reliability coefficient anticipated if the test were doubled in length and r_s is the reliability coefficient calculated using the shortened halves of the original test. If, for example, $r_s = 0.50$, then $r_1 = 0.67$.

Many shortcut methods for estimating the reliability of a test have been produced over the past 50 years. Some of these require either the calculation or estimation of the standard deviation of the scores. For the classroom teacher, the most practical of such formulas would seem to be Diederich's[1] modification of the Kuder-Richardson Formula 21. This formula is given as

$$r = 1 - \frac{M(K - M)}{Ks^2},$$ (2.2)

where M is the mean of the test scores, K is the number of items in the test, and s^2 is the variance (or squared standard deviation) of the test scores.

Obviously, the only two values which need be calculated to enter this formula are the mean and variance of the test scores. How to calculate these two entities will be explained in a later section of this book.

If the teacher calculates the reliability coefficient of one of his tests, what can he expect to find? To be reasonably acceptable, the reliability coefficient should be at least 0.60. A very good reliability coefficient for the typical classroom test would be 0.80. If the test does not

[1] Paul B. Diederich, *Shortcut Statistics for Teacher-Made Tests* (Educational Testing Service, Princeton, N. J., 1964).

reach a reliability of 0.60, the procedure of item analysis, which will be described later, can be used to increase its reliability.

ESTIMATING RELEVANCE

There are two methods of estimating the relevance of a test, only one of which is normally applicable to classroom achievement tests. The first method is generally called *empirical relevance*; the second is called *logical relevance*. It is the latter approach which is more appropriate for classroom tests, but the teacher should also have some understanding of the meaning of empirical relevance.

Empirical relevance. When we attempt to establish empirical relevance for a test, we must demonstrate an observed relationship between the scores on that test and another set of scores called *criterion* scores. Such criterion scores serve as an outside, or independent measure of the function or variable we are attempting to measure with our own test. As an example, let us assume that I am attempting to construct a new, short method for measuring intelligence. As part of my test validation procedure I would probably administer both my test and some well-known individual intelligence test, such as the Stanford-Binet, to the same group of individuals. The IQ's derived from the Stanford-Binet would serve as the criterion scores. I would attempt to demonstrate by correlation coefficient that the scores on my test were reasonably highly related to the criterion scores. If they were, I could assert that my test was relevant because the measures it produces are in substantial agreement with other, independent measures of the same thing.

Estimating relevance by empirical methods is most frequently encountered in the validation procedures for intelligence, aptitude, or personality tests. It is not used with achievement tests because of the difficulty of finding appropriate criterion scores. If, for example, you are constructing a test to cover a unit in biology which you have just finished teaching, where would you find another test which would provide an independent and more relevant measure of the same achievement? Even a standardized test would be a less relevant measure because it would cover a broader area than you would wish, and it would fail to take into account any novel or unique characteristics of the local curriculum. We must ruefully conclude that the teacher's test itself is the most relevant measure available of the particular achievement we wish to measure. When this is the case, we must approach relevance through logical rather than empirical means.

Logical relevance. When we attempt to demonstrate the relevance of a test by logical means, we must demonstrate that the contents of that test will elicit the types of behavior specified in our statements of objectives. That is, the test must require the student to perform those types of operations which we wish him to be able to perform, and he must be able to respond successfully, insofar as possible, only by the appropriate use of those operations and not by other means. To the extent that the test content does not accurately reflect our objectives and to the extent that student responses may, in part, be determined by factors other than the prescribed achievement, the test lacks relevance.

Unlike empirical relevance, there is no numerical estimate of relevance when logical analysis is employed. Hence, it is impossible for the teacher to obtain a numerical estimate of the validity of the test using methods described in books on measurement theory. This, however, need not be a matter of great concern for the teacher. If he can demonstrate by logical means that his test is relevant, and if the calculated reliability coefficient for the test is reasonably high, he can be assured that his test is valid.

FACTORS AFFECTING VALIDITY

The exact relationships among the three factors of validity, reliability, and relevance can best be illustrated through a consideration of factors affecting the magnitude of these three qualities of a measuring instrument. As we shall see, the effect of most of these factors is to introduce a certain amount of error into the readings we obtain from an instrument. Let us begin with the example of a simple type of measurement and then generalize to the measurement of educational achievement.

When a individual stands on a bathroom scale, the *score* that he reads (the number of pounds) will be determined only in part by his actual weight at the time. The score will also be affected by the amount and type of clothing he is wearing and by the weight of the things he is carrying in his pockets. The condition of the scale itself will influence the score. The adjustment may be inaccurate, or the scale may be inclined to stick. Since most bathroom scales measure the effect of weight on the expansion of a spring, and since that expansion is affected by variations in temperature, the score will be dependent in part upon the temperature of the room. Similarly, the age of the scale and the amount of use it has had may influence the reading of the number of pounds. Again, the position the individual takes in standing on the scale and his angle of sight may have an effect. Even the individual's attitude about his weight (whether he considers himself overweight or underweight) may be reflected in the score he reads. The influence of any of these extraneous factors may be slight, but to the extent that they operate they introduce *errors of measurement* into the weight which the individual reads from the scale.

SOURCES OF VARIABILITY IN TEST SCORES

As has been indicated, any test score will reflect the influence of a wide variety of factors. These factors make one person's score different from another person's score, or they make the score obtained by an individual at one time under certain conditions different from the score that he would obtain at another time under different conditions. For example, consider the scores obtained from the administration of a test consisting of a number of problems in arithmetic. A pupil's score on this test will be determined in part by his skill in addition, subtraction, multiplication, and division. The score will also be influenced by the pupil's ability to analyze the problem and to select the appropriate processes to apply in the solution. The ability to select between pertinent and unnecessary information may be involved. Intelligence and reading ability will undoubtedly affect the score, as will the pupil's motivation toward success. The student's health and physical condition, the temperature, lighting, ventilation, and general condition of the room, the presence of distracting noises—all these and many other factors may influence the performance of the pupil.

The influence of some of the factors affecting a test score will be *temporary*. Some conditions may change from minute to minute, hour to hour, or day to day. The factors associated with the room in which the test is given certainly fall in this class. The condition of the individual's health varies from day to day. Emotional tension, mood, and fatigue are temporary factors which may influence the test score.

In comparison to these, the influence of other factors is relatively *lasting*. The individual's ability to perform the basic arithmetic processes, his ability to analyze problems, his intelligence, and his reading ability do not change drastically from one day to the next. It should be noted that here *lasting* does not necessarily mean *permanent*. Many of the relatively lasting factors which influence the test score (such as reading ability) are subject to change, but the change occurs slowly over a considerable period of time. The pupil does not learn to read overnight, nor is he likely to make a marked improvement in reading ability in so short a time.

In addition to the consideration of whether the factor is a temporary or lasting one, we can recognize that the influence of some factors is determined by *chance*. On any item requiring the pupil to select his response from among possible answers which are presented to him (the multiple-choice item), the individual may succeed on the basis of a "blind," or random, guess.[2] The influence of such guesses on the test score is determined by chance. The distinguishing characteristic of a *chance factor* is that its effect on the test score is unpredictable. If we know that a student has responded to every item on a true-false test by making a random guess, we cannot predict whether his score will be high or low. We can predict the distribution of a large number of scores determined by such guesses, and on the basis of that distribution we can establish the probability of an individual's obtaining any given score. But we cannot predict the exact score that a given individual will obtain at any given time.

A second illustration of a chance factor, closely related to the first, is the general tendency of the individual to "take a chance." Some students refuse to respond to any item unless they are reasonably certain of the answer. Some will omit items if they do not know the answer, even when they are urged to guess. Other students will guess on items even when they are informed that they will be penalized for wrong guesses. They are willing to run the risk of the penalty on the chance of guessing the answer. The tendency to take a chance is a lasting characteristic of the individual, but its effect on the test score is determined by chance whenever the guesses are made at random.

Another example of a chance factor is that which arises in the selection of the particular items to be included in the test. Theoretically no student could answer all of the items which might possibly be written for a given test. In writing the particular test, we may include a disproportionate number of items which the individual can answer, or conversely we may include a disproportionate number of items which

---

[2] A distinction needs to be made between this kind of "blind" guessing and what may be called "considered" or "enlightened" guessing. Most of the guessing that occurs in the test situation is of this second type. What the individual means when he reports that he guessed the answer to a particular item is that he answered with something less than certainty, but on the basis of partial knowledge or hunches. He may have eliminated with a high degree of confidence all but two of the alternative responses and then guessed (again generally on the basis of partial knowledge). The influence of such "enlightened" guesses is certainly not determined by chance.

the individual cannot answer. To the extent that chance determines the inclusion of particular items, the effect of this selection of items is unpredictable.

While chance probably plays at least a small part in determining the scores on any test, most of the factors which affect test scores have a *systematic* influence. Theoretically, the influence of these systematic factors is predictable. If we know that a given factor is operating and if we know the effect of that factor on the performance of each individual, we could predict the influence of that factor on each individual's score. For example, if the score on a test depends in part upon reading ability, and if the influence of all other factors is equal for two students, then the better reader will receive the higher score on the test.

On the basis of these considerations, the various factors which influence a test score (or the application of any measuring device) can be classified into one of the four cells in a chart such as is given in Table 2.1. Some of the factors will be lasting and systematic, some temporary and systematic, some lasting and chance, and some temporary and chance. We can conceive of the score which a pupil obtains on the test as the sum of his scores for each of the various factors which influence his performance.

Our primary concern in the measurement of educational achievement is with our objectives. This means that we are concerned with lasting characteristics of the individual.[3] It follows, then, that the influence of temporary factors must introduce errors of measurement into our measures of achievement. Since we are interested in predicting future behavior on the basis of present performance, we are concerned with systematic factors. Chance factors, therefore, also introduce errors of measurement. In addition, some of the lasting and systematic factors which the test measures may have nothing to do with the particular

---

[3] Occasionally, and in special circumstances, we may be concerned with the measurement of a factor whose influence varies rather rapidly. Special problems are presented in such cases. Our concern here is with educational achievement. Therefore, discussion will be limited to the measurement of lasting factors.

TABLE 2.1 CLASSIFICATION OF SOURCES OF VARIABILITY IN TEST SCORES.[a]

	Lasting Factors	Temporary Factors
Systematic factors	Level of ability on trait or traits required by test	Skill with particular item form
	Intelligence	Health
	Reading ability (general comprehension of instructions)	Fatigue
		Motivation (at the moment)
		Emotional strain
	General motivation toward success	External conditions such as: Heat
	Physical handicap, such as: Hearing loss Poor eyesight	Lighting Ventilation Test administrator
	Ability to work with speed	Factors operating on the test scorer: Bias Fatigue Emotional strain External conditions Level of ability
Chance factors	General tendency to take a chance	"Chance" in whether the individual knows or does not the answer to the item (sampling of items)
		"Luck" in guessing answers

[a]This list of factors is merely suggestive of the very wide variety of factors which might operate to influence test scores.

aspect of achievement with which the test is concerned. For example, on an arithmetic test we may not be concerned with the individual's reading ability. In this case, to the extent that it influences the test score, reading ability introduces an error of measurement.

If we could identify and eliminate all such errors of measurement from our test score, we would have left a perfect measure of the characteristic with which we are concerned. For each individual, we could obtain his "true" score on the characteristic. Such a perfect measure is, of course, impossible for reasons which have already been presented. We can assume that such a true score exists, however, and that the test score obtained by an individual is the algebraic sum of his true score plus scores for the various error factors. Some of these error scores will increase the test score, while others will depress it. That is, some of the error scores will be positive while others will be negative. In theory, we will pool the effects of all lasting and systematic errors into one error score, and we will pool the effects of all temporary and/or chance factors into a second error score. The obtained score for any person is made up in part from his true score, in part from a score for systematic and lasting errors, and in part from a score for temporary and/or chance errors. This relationship may be expressed by the equation

$$S = T + e_1 + e_2,$$

where S is an individual's obtained score, T is his true score, e_1 is the influence of lasting and systematic errors of measurement, and e_2 is the influence of temporary and/or chance errors.

Figure 2.2   The division of a test score into its "true" score and error components.

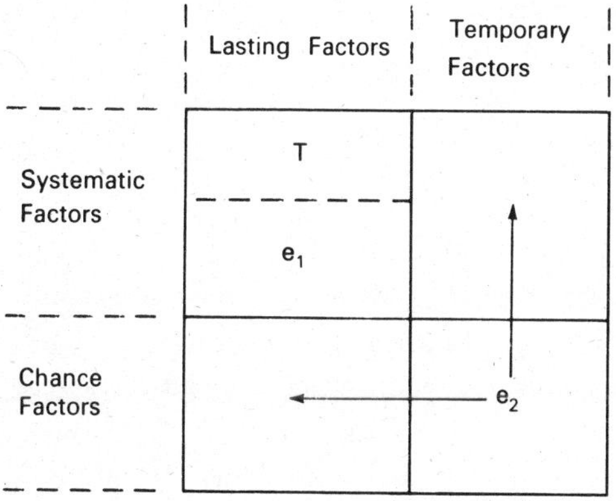

The relationship may also be presented in the form of a diagram. Using a chart similar to that presented in Table 2.1, we can let the total area of the chart represent the obtained score on the test. We will divide the lasting and systematic factors into two parts. One part will include those factors contributing to the true score, and the other will include the lasting and systematic errors of measurement. Now the total area has been divided into its true score and error components, as shown in Figure 2.2.

Figure 2.1 gives the impression that most of the test score is the result of errors of measurement. It is certainly to be hoped that this will not be the case. A more desirable division of a test score into its true score and error components is illustrated in Figure 2.3.

Figure 2.3 A more desirable division of a test score into its components.

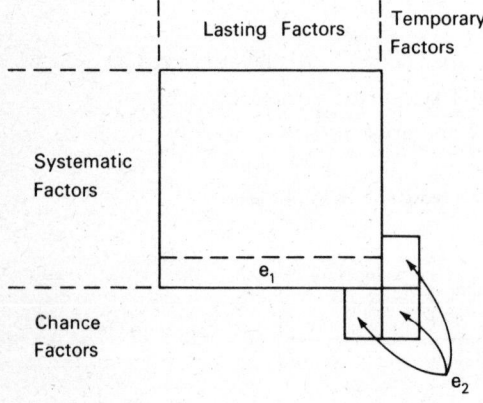

VALIDITY

The *validity* of a test is the consistency with which the test measures the trait (or traits) which it is used to measure. There are two parts to this definition: (1) "the consistency with which the test measures" and (2) the degree "to which the test measures the trait (or traits) which it is used to measure." To be valid, the test should be consistent in the scores that it gives. If we can assume that the individual has not changed with regard to the trait measured, a valid test should give the same score for that individual on each of several administrations. This consistency of a test score is designated by the term *reliability*. The degree to which the test measures the trait (or traits) which it is used to measure is the *relevance*[4] of the test. The validity of a test, then, is dependent upon its relevance and its reliability. To have some degree of validity, the test must have some degree of both relevance and reliability. A test that is completely lacking in either relevance or reliability can have no validity. To be perfectly valid (which no test can be, since perfect measurement is impossible), a test would have to be both perfectly relevant and perfectly reliable.

We can approach the concept of validity through a consideration of errors of measurement. As has been indicated, we can improve the quality of a test score by identifying sources of error and eliminating (or decreasing) their influence on the score. The *quality* which is being improved is, by definition, the validity of the test. The validity, then, is inversely related to the influence of all errors of measurement, both lasting and systematic errors (e_1) and temporary and/or chance errors (e_2). If the influence of all errors of measurement could be eliminated, the test score would be the true score, and the test would be perfectly valid. In this hypothetical case of a perfectly valid test, our equation for the obtained score becomes

$$S = T,$$

since e_1 and e_2 have been reduced to zero. Therefore, we can also define the validity of a test as the degree of relationship between the test scores and the corresponding true scores. This definition is consistent

---

[4] See E. E. Cureton, in *Educational Measurement*, edited by E. F. Lindquist (American Council on Education, Washington, 1951), chapter 16. The present discussion follows Cureton's in distinguishing relevance as contributing to validity. Prior to Cureton, the term *validity* was sometimes used to designate relevance and at other times was used to indicate both relevance and reliability.

with the previous one, and both definitions are consistent with the statement that the best test (that is, the most valid test) is the one which most closely approaches the criterion series.

RELEVANCE

The *relevance* of a test is the degree to which the trait(s) which the test measures agree, or are related to, the trait(s) which the test is used to measure. It is important to note that the relevance of a test must be judged in terms of the use that is made of the test. A test may be highly relevant in one situation, but less relevant, or completely irrelevant, in another situation. A relevant test of arithmetic skills would have little relevance as a measure of achievement in U. S. history. A relevant test of achievement in a college course in U. S. history would be less relevant if used at the high-school level. A test designed to measure the knowledge and understanding of current events may be relevant today, but in ten years it will no longer be relevant as a current events test. We are concerned, then, with whether or not the test is relevant to (1) the purpose for which it is used, (2) the group with which it is used, and (3) the time at which it is used.

Relevance is inversely related to the influence of lasting and systematic errors on the test score. The less the effect of such errors, the greater will be the relevance of the test. With a perfectly relevant measuring device, all of the lasting and systematic factors which influence the score will pertain to the characteristic being measured. In this case, the score for lasting and systematic errors of measurement would be zero, and our formula for the test score would become

$S = T + e_2$.

A perfectly relevant test is possible whenever the measuring device is used to define the characteristic measured. A yardstick is a perfectly relevant measure of distance, since a yard is the distance covered by the stick. If we distinguish between *intelligence* and *IQ* and define IQ as the characteristic measured by the Stanford-Binet Scale, we might question the relevance of the Stanford-Binet Scale as a measure of intelligence, but there is no question as to its relevance as a measure of IQ.

RELIABILITY

The *reliability* of a test is the consistency with which the test measures whatever it does measure. A reliable test tends to give the same score to the same individual on each of several administrations. A test may be highly reliable even though the characteristic which it measures (whatever it does measure) has nothing to do with the purpose for which the test is used. Reliability refers only to the consistency of the scores obtained for the same individuals on successive administrations of the measuring device. This meaning of the term reliability in describing a quality of a test is somewhat more limited than the meaning of the term in its general application. When we say that a person is reliable in keeping appointments, we generally mean that he is consistently on time. Consider, however, the individual who is never on time for an appointment, but who always arrives fifteen minutes late. No one could argue that this person is punctual, but we can point out that, in one sense, he is reliable. We can rely on him to be fifteen minutes late. In this sense, the individual who is always fifteen minutes late is as reliable as the individual who is always on time. His reliability depends upon the consistency of his behavior, not necessarily on its accuracy. It is in this sense that we speak of the reliability of a test.

Considering the factors which affect a test score, we can note that it is the influence of temporary and chance factors which will cause a person's score to be different on one occasion from what his score would have been had the test been given on a different occasion. The reliability of a test, then, is inversely related to the influence of temporary and/or chance errors of measurement. A perfectly reliable test would be one on which the influence of all temporary and/or chance factors had been completely eliminated. Such a situation is possible only in theory. A more precise statement would be that no measure is perfectly reliable, since it is impossible to eliminate entirely the influence of temporary and/or chance factors. However, in the hypothetical case of a perfectly reliable test, our formula for the obtained score would become

$$S = T + e_1,$$

or

$$S = e_1.$$

In the case of the second formula, the test score would be exclusively the result of lasting and systematic errors of measurement. Theoretically, then, a test score could be completely irrelevant and yet perfectly reliable.[5]

MATHEMATICAL RELATIONSHIP AMONG VALIDITY, RELIABILITY, AND RELEVANCE

As we indicated earlier in this chapter, the coefficient of correlation is normally used as an index of the magnitude of the validity, reliability, or relevance of a test. In the case of relevance, of course, this will be true only where criterion scores are available. Assuming this to be the case, it can be demonstrated that the coefficient of validity of a test is equal to the product of the coefficient of relevance and the square root of the reliability coefficient. In algebraic terms,[6]

$$r_v = r_{..} \sqrt{r_{xx}} \tag{2.3}$$

---

[5] On the other hand, a perfectly relevant but completely unreliable test is impossible even in theory. To be completely unreliable, all of the variation in test scores would have to be due to temporary and/or chance errors. If this were the case, there could be no systematic and lasting variation. Thus, there could be no true score.

[6] The mathematical derivation of this formula is given in the Appendix.

where r_v is the coefficient of validity or the correlation coefficient between the test score and a perfectly reliable criterion, $r..$ is the coefficient of relevance or the correlation between a perfectly reliable test score and a perfectly reliable criterion, and r_{xx} is the reliability coefficient of the test.

We should, of course, attempt to make our measures as valid as possible. While the teacher should be aware of factors which negatively influence the reliability and try to minimize their influence, he generally has greater control over factors related to relevance. Most of the content of this book is aimed at improving the relevance of teacher-made tests and other types of instruments for measuring student achievement. This is particularly true of those portions dealing with topics such as the specification of test content, the writing of test items and the errors to be avoided, the writing of appropriate directions, the timing of tests, and the appropriateness of the test for the group tested.

We must end this chapter with a note of warning, however. Validity is always specific, never general. That is, a test may be valid in one situation for one group of students but not in another situation with another group of students. However, so long as the students in the teacher's classes remain much the same, so long as the objectives remain the same, and so long as the relevance of the test items is not abraded by excessive exposure to successive generations of such students, a well-constructed test will probably remain valid for some time.

3
EDUCATIONAL
OBJECTIVES

B efore a teacher can begin to devise any sort of instrument to measure educational *achievement,* he must decide what it is that he wishes to measure. What he wishes to measure will define what he means by achievement. To the extent that the teacher has a clear conception of what he wishes to measure, he has solved one of the basic problems of educational measurement.

Unfortunately, most teachers lack such a clear conception because they have never given sufficient thought to the matter. They assume that the problem of test content is a fairly simple one. All one needs to do is ask questions and present problems based on "what has been covered," and any achievement test will have prima facie validity. Unfortunately, the problem of test validity is not that simple.

Most teachers would, on reflection, be willing to admit that what they cover as the content of their instruction does not exactly coincide with their instructional aims. They know very well that of all the things which are learned in school, specific information is most readily forgotten. The most permanent learnings are certain types of skills, understandings, and insights. The ability to use such skills, understandings, and insights in new situations is the very essence of education. To accept this position, however, is not to derogate information entirely. The possession of useful information is essential to an educated citizen, and the more information an individual has immediately at hand, the better educationally prepared he may be assumed to be. But information is not education, and the teacher always knows this.

The teacher must be willing to ask the searching question: "What is it that I really hope to accomplish by my teaching?" Phrased in other ways, he might ask: "What is it that I am about?" Or: "What are the prime purposes of my teaching that are peculiar to my grade or subject and that I can hope to accomplish in the time allotted to me?" When he begins to ask questions such as these, he has begun the search for meaningful educational objectives.

It should be made clear, at this point, that the ability to formulate and state explicit educational objectives is not a necessary prelude to or a condition of excellent teaching. There are many master teachers who have never made explicit the precise goals they hope to accomplish. The force of their personalities and the imagination and vigor of their procedures are such that we do not question the generalities in which their aims are couched. To do so would seem an affront to a recognizably competent individual. Yet, it must be apparent that though good teaching may flourish under such conditions, good measurement cannot. The two are not necessary concomitants. Many excellent teachers devise inferior tests. They do so because they are unwilling to divert any appreciable portion of their tremendous talent from the problems of teaching to the problems of measurement.

This is an unfortunate situation because the two problems do naturally go together. A rigorous analysis of one's teaching aims can have a tremendously salutary effect upon one's teaching. It can help an individual to decide which instructional outcomes are really most important and which ones he can really hope to accomplish. If, in addition, he can convey this information to his students so they, too, know his aims, many of his more difficult instructional problems may be solved, or at least ameliorated. But this will happen only if objectives can be stated in the proper way.

The proper way to state educational objectives, from the point of view of educational measurement, is to specify the behavior one would be able to observe in the student if he had, in fact, accomplished this objective. In other words, what is it that he would now be able to do which he could not do prior to instruction? If a teacher can specify such behavior, then he can arrange for the behavior to be exhibited under controlled or structured conditions.

Upon reflection, it should be apparent that this is really the only way in which we ever do assess achievement of any kind. If we judge that a person is a good playwright (high on achievement in writing plays), we base our judgment on the fact that he writes good plays. Now we may not see him in the actual process of writing the play. In fact, we may not be terribly interested in whether he writes his original drafts in longhand, uses a recording machine, or dictates them to a secretary. We judge the product which we know (or think we know) is the result of the author's creative process. Since product and process are inextricably bound together, we can define a good playwright as one who writes good plays. Were we teaching a course in playwriting, we would be perfectly willing to accept the product as evidence of the process if we had assurance that the product was original. In other situations, judgment of achievement based on observation of behavior is more apparent than in the case of the playwright. If we call in a TV repairman, we judge his effectiveness both on his behavior and his results. If he were able to eliminate the ills of our set by waving a wand in front of the picture tube, we might be properly impressed, but would likely switch our business to another agency in the future. Despite the undoubted efficiency of his method, his unorthodox behavior would not inspire our confidence.

What we must recognize is that we are always making inferences about the competency of persons based on their behavior. We infer that a person is a good mechanic because his behavior is such as to produce a lasting impression on the engine of our car. We infer that another person is intelligent because he makes witty or trenchant remarks. Similarly, we infer that a student has learned if he is now able to do the things which he was unable to do prior to instruction. But note that mechanical ability, intelligence, learning, and achievement are all inferences from observed behavior or from the outcome of such behavior. They are, themselves, never directly observed. For that matter, there is no way of our knowing empirically whether such processes really exist. The question of the reality of such processes is not, however, central to our discussion. What is central is the recognition that the measurement of any type of achievement is based upon an observation of process (or behavior), product (or outcome), or some combination of the two.

The analysis of educational aims, therefore, should begin with the specification of those processes or products which define achievement in the area in which we are teaching. This will ensure that what we eventually measure will be as closely related to what we intend to measure as we can possibly make it.

As we shall discuss in the next chapter, this is the problem of maximizing the relevance of a measuring instrument.

THE PROCESS OF FORMULATING OBJECTIVES

Upon beginning an analysis of his teaching goals, the typical teacher will start with statements of what it is the students should know. The history teacher will say, for example, that his students should know the generally accepted causes of World War I and should know the names and achievements of the leaders of the major national powers of that era. The physical education teacher will say that his students should know how to play basketball, how to keep physically fit, and how to accept defeat gracefully. The primary school teacher will say that her students should know how to read, how to write the letters of the alphabet, and how to add two one-digit numbers. All such statements seem perfectly logical and in keeping with the apparent responsibilities of the respective teachers.

But it is easy to mistake the type of statements which have been made for the root meaning of achievement. Take, for example, the statement that students should know the generally accepted causes of World War I. What does it mean to "know" in the sense in which the word is used here? How can I tell when a student "knows" this information? What set of operations would enable me to distinguish between those students who know and those who do not know? What would a student have to be able to do so I could assert with some degree of confidence that he "knows" the causes of World War I? Would I accept a verbal listing in response to a direct question? Would I insist upon a written listing, or would I settle for the ability to select the correct causes from a list which also included incorrect answers? These three behaviors are not the same, and each might be said to represent a different type of "ability" or "knowledge." It is entirely possible that a student could do one and be unable to do the others.

We could even ask the same questions about one of the more precise statements offered—the ability to add two one-digit numbers. On first examination, this statement seems reasonably clear. We might attempt to reformulate it, however, and ask the teacher if this is not more clearly what she meant. Our statement might read: "When presented with two one-digit numbers in the form $\begin{array}{r} 9 \\ +6 \\ \hline \end{array}$ the student is able to write the correct sum below the line in at least eight out of ten trials." Our teacher might object, however, and say this was only part of what she intended. She also meant that he should be able to solve such problems when they are presented in the form $9 + 6 = $ _____ . In addition, he should be able to respond successfully to the same problem presented in this form: "If John had nine marbles and his brother gave him six more, how many marbles would he have altogether?" At this point, the teacher should become aware that more is involved in the latter form of presentation than simply the ability to add 6 to 9. For one thing, the student must realize, after reading the item, that this is a problem which calls for the use of the additive process. We could say that he must be able to "apply" his knowledge of addition to a problem of this type. This, obviously, is a somewhat higher level of achievement than simply adding 6 to 9.

So we can see that almost any statement we are likely to make initially as a proposed objective can be further refined. The refinement must proceed to the point where we are willing to say: "Yes, this is what I really meant by that statement." Obviously, there is a point of diminishing returns in this process. In the example of arithmetic, there would be no point in specifying such trivial conditions as the type of paper or pencil, the necessity for "lining up" the answer with the digits in the problem, and so forth. We need to refine our statements only to the point where it becomes clear exactly what we must do in order to observe whether the student can or cannot perform as the objective specifies. A well-stated objective should point clearly to the type of task which *must* be set before the student so he may demonstrate his possession or lack of possession of the relevant achievement. The teacher knows then what he *must* do in designing an appropriate technique to measure this achievement: He must include tasks of this type. The remaining job is to decide upon the format in which these tasks will be presented and the content in which they will be embedded.

One of the best treatments of the problem of formulating behavioral objectives for the classroom is to be found in a short programmed textbook by Mager.[1] Mager gives a step-by-step approach to the writing of

---

[1] R. E. Mager, *Preparing Instructional Objectives* (Feron Publishers, Inc., Palo Alto, Calif., 1962).

such objectives, and also gives examples of what *not* to do. He lists three characteristics of a well-formulated objective:

1. It identifies and names the overall behavior act.
2. It defines the important conditions under which the behavior is to occur (givens or restrictions, or both).
3. It defines the criterion of acceptable performance.

Note that the objective regarding primary arithmetic which we presented on the previous page follows Mager's specification. The initial part of the sentence ("when presented with two one-digit numbers in the form $+\frac{9}{6}$ . . .") sets the conditions for the behavior. The middle part of the sentence (". . . the student is able to write the correct sum below the line . . .") specifies the behavior which is to be observed. The last part of the sentence (". . . in at least eight out of ten trials.") defines the criterion of acceptable performance.

Mager warns against the use of such expressions as "to know," "to understand," or "to appreciate," as specifications of behavior. These expressions refer to essentially unobservable acts, and the words are open to many interpretations. More acceptable expressions because they are open to fewer interpretations, from Mager's view, are "to list," "to solve," and "to construct." If objectives can be formulated using expressions such as the latter set, then unbiased and independent observers could view the behavior and agree whether students were or were not exhibiting the type of performance specified. In addition, we who write such objectives will be specifying exactly what we mean by "achievement" in the area covered by this objective, and our meaning is likely to be clear to anyone willing to read such objectives carefully.

Defining outcomes strictly in terms of observable behavior has one drawback, however. It does not adequately cover those aspects of achievement where it is product, not process, that is important. We have previously alluded to the case of creative writing where the mode and manner of the process are distinctly secondary to the product. The same is true of items presented on most objectively scored tests. If the answer sheets are to be machine scored, the only behavior which can be observed in the student while he is performing the task is an occasional vertical movement of his pencil. The crucial behavior in such instances is unobservable because it occurs "inside" the student. It is the product, in this case the pattern of marks on the answer sheet, which is important to us because it provides us with the necessary data for making inferences about the unobservable process. In cases such as these, outcomes need to be defined in terms of the type of task presented to the student rather than in terms of the behavior which is to be observed. It is here that a different approach to defining objectives becomes useful.

This second approach is best illustrated by reference to Bloom, *Taxonomy of Educational Objectives*.[2] There are currently two volumes of this handbook. The first is devoted to the cognitive domain and the second to the affective domain. It is the first volume which has most relevance for our discussion. We may consider the "unseen" behaviors referred to in the previous paragraph as cognitive behaviors. What Bloom and his associates have done is to classify such cognitive behaviors in six levels. The behaviors in the higher levels are assumed to depend upon prior acquisition of the behaviors at the lower levels. The six levels are:

1. Knowledge
2. Comprehension
3. Application
4. Analysis
5. Synthesis
6. Evaluation

Bloom gives many examples of the types of tasks or test items which can be used to measure behaviors at each of the six levels. It is not necessary, of course, that all six levels be used in any given test. As a

[2]Benjamin S. Bloom, *Taxonomy of Educational Objectives* (Longmans, Green and Co., New York, 1956).

matter of fact, at the beginning levels of instruction in any given subject, it is unlikely that a test would go beyond the first three levels of the taxonomy.

The two approaches to this statement of objectives represented by Mager and Bloom can be combined if it is clearly understood that the behaviors to which Bloom refers are cognitive behaviors. For example, we might take an objective which conceivably could have been formulated by a teacher of the social sciences in a high school:

Given a graph which presents information on some economic trend in the recent history of the U.S., the student can interpret this graph with sufficient accuracy to classify a series of propositions relevant to the graph in the following fashion:

1. The proposition is definitely true.
2. The proposition is probably true.
3. The proposition is probably false.
4. The proposition is definitely false.
5. The information given is not sufficient to indicate any degree of truth or falsity in the proposition.

Such a task would fall at the level of "interpretation" in the Bloom taxonomy. Note that the objective states the conditions (the givens) under which the student is to perform. Although the behavior of interpretation is essentially unobservable, the behavior of classification is not. But, it is likely that we would not be simply interested in observing the student while he made his classifications. These would probably consist of marks placed in one of the five possible response positions on an answer sheet. More likely, we would be interested only in the final outcome, the classifications he produced. Note also that no "criterion of acceptable performance" is specified, as Mager suggests. In most cognitive tasks where any evaluations of performance are likely to be made on a relative basis, it is difficult to specify ahead of time exactly how well a student should be expected to perform. This difficulty leads testmakers to produce two different types of tests depending upon the type of objective employed. These two types of tests are called *criterion-referenced* and *norm-referenced* tests.

CRITERION-REFERENCED VERSUS NORM-REFERENCED TESTS

When we discussed the matter of stating educational objectives in behavioral form and set forth the requirements for such statements as given by Mager, we said that one of the requirements was that the statement should define the criterion of acceptable performance. We gave as an example the statement: "When presented with two one-digit numbers in the form $+\underline{6}^{9}$, the student is able to write the correct sum below the line in at least eight out of ten trials." The last part of the statement ("... in at least eight out of ten trials.") defines the criterion of acceptable performance. If the student performs at this or a higher level, he is judged to have met the objective. If he fails to perform at this level, he has not met the objective. It is our anticipation, however, that with further instruction, he, too, will be able to perform at this acceptable level.

The basic idea underlying the so-called *criterion-referenced* test (or *mastery* test) is that the test is composed of tasks or items for which a clearly definable criterion of successful performance is available. Generally, this criterion is stated as a certain proportion or percentage of the items on the test, such as 80 percent. This criterion is selected in advance of administration of the test largely on the basis of the judgment of the testmaker as he reflects his experience with previous generations of students learning this material. Typically, the criterion is set as something less than perfect performance to allow for a certain measure of unreliability in student performance.

The expectation under mastery testing is that if the objectives are clearly stated and are made known to the students prior to instruction, all students will eventually meet the criterion. Differences among students will take the form of differences in time needed to achieve the criterion. Differences in final performance will be minimized.

Mastery testing assumes a known, finite set of specific objectives which are to be mastered. The 100 basic addition facts form one such set. We can determine mastery of these facts as evidenced by successful performance of the objective, as previously stated. As the set of potential objectives becomes large and the possible operations which define their achievement increase, the idea of mastery becomes less applicable if not completely meaningless. We may be able to agree on what is meant by mastery of arithmetic; mastery of history is not so clear. In fact one might well argue that mastery of the complex field of history is impossible; the more one learns of the field the more he realizes how much he does not know. In these cases, we are frequently forced to evaluate achievement on a relative basis through norm-referenced tests.

In the case of norm-referenced tests, our expectation is that we will maximize differences in student performance. The norm-referenced test is sometimes called the test of *relative achievement*. Its purpose is to place students as accurately as possible somewhere along the range of possible achievement for the test from the very lowest to the very highest scores. Most students will fall somewhere in the middle giving us a distribution of scores somewhat resembling the so-called *normal* distribution.

Most tests of relative achievement are based on educational objectives phrased as cognitive behaviors. Items are written that are relevant to these objectives. These items tend to be both positively discriminating and moderately difficult.[3] If these two conditions are met, the scores obtained from such a test will yield the maximum variability among students and the largest possible range of scores.

Tests of relative achievement are most frequently used for purposes of assigning grades to students. It is difficult to assign grades if all students

[3]The concepts of discriminating power and difficulty will be developed in Chapter 7.

perform at the same or nearly the same level. A simple pass-fail or satisfactory-unsatisfactory dichotomy seems most appropriate to such a situation. If further refinement is required, however, the test of relative achievement will provide more information than the mastery test. It is obvious, however, that both types of tests will be useful to the classroom teacher.

How many objectives should a teacher write for a given unit of instruction, for a term, or for a year? There is no exact answer to this question. He should write as many as reasonable and necessary. What he must do is to begin by stating in general terms what he believes to be the most important outcomes of his instruction. This will depend largely on his own professional judgment, although he may be assisted in this process by statements made by some of the professional associations for teachers, such as the National Council of Teachers of English or the National Science Teachers Association. Having stated his aims in a general fashion, he can then proceed to refine these statements in the manner we have described previously. From such refined statements he can cull those which now seem relatively unimportant or which seem incapable of measurement in any meaningful way. The remaining statements will serve to define what he means by "achievement" in his teaching area and can be used as directives to the type of measuring instruments he must construct in order to measure such achievement. How to construct such instruments is a major concern of this book.

4
OBSERVATIONAL TESTS

Mention the word "test" to almost anyone, and he typically thinks of a student sitting at a desk, paper and pencil in front of him, ready to match wits with a series of questions posed by some teacher. This is what the word has come to mean in recent years, but it is interesting to note that the first "tests" were not of this sort. Etymologically, the word was originally applied to the assessment of certain products, as, for example, a test for the purity of gold. It was also applied to performances. The tasks required of the young boy about to enter manhood in the many forms of puberty rites can also be considered an early form of testing. The test was essentially a sort of "crucial trial" where the product or performance was subjected to close scrutiny to determine its worth. The original meaning of the word is still maintained in many facets of daily life. We test the stage of recovery of a sprained ankle by gently lowering our weight on it. We test a guitar string to see if it is in tune. Laboratory and clinical tests of all sorts exemplify the original meaning. Despite the historical primacy of this type of test, however, paper-and-pencil tests, though not a recent introduction (the Chinese used them 2000 years ago), have dominated school achievement testing for the past 100 years. We should not allow this situation to blind us to the fact that the older type of test may still possess considerable validity for assessing school achievement.

Basically, there are two types of tests typically employed in measuring school achievement. The first is the familiar paper-and-pencil test alluded to in the previous paragraph. The second is the now less familiar but historically more fundamental observational test. We should note that the word "observational" here is something of a misnomer. Actually, any type of test is an observation in the technical sense. When we speak of making "observations," as in an educational experiment, we frequently mean the obtaining of a number of measures on subjects through the use of some type of test. Thus a paper-and-pencil test is observational in the sense that we make observations through its use. However, by custom, the observational test or observational *technique* as it is sometimes called, has come to refer to certain specific measuring devices.

The observational test differs from the paper-and-pencil test in two major ways. First, it is normally used on only one student at a time. The paper-and-pencil test may be used on only one student, but it is uneconomical to do so. Usually we test all the members of a class simultaneously when we use paper-and-pencil tests. Second, when employing an observational test, the teacher does the recording. When using paper-and-pencil tests, the student normally does the recording.

There are many types of important school achievements that are not amenable to assessment with a paper-and-pencil test. Included among such achievements would be the various physical skills, many of the verbal skills, and some of the mental skills. As an example, take the ability to speak in front of the class. If we were to attempt to test this ability by means of a paper-and-pencil test we might discover whether the student knew the principles of good delivery, whether he could recognize errors in organization of speech materials, or whether he could write an effective opening. We would still not know whether he could give a good speech. The only way we can determine this is to listen to him as he speaks and then make some assessment of his performance.

Actually, much of the time of the teacher is spent in making observations of student performance. A job analysis of the role of the teacher would show that he is listening to students, watching them perform, and making judgments about the quality of their performance. Most of this is done in an unsystematic fashion, and the teacher would be hard put to cite specific evidence supporting the judgments he makes. The teacher should not necessarily be criticized for this, because his job is a very demanding one, and all too frequently he has neither the time nor the inclination to be systematic in his observations. However, in any class, there are certain crucial types of achievement which should be assessed systematically. These are the ones specified by the teacher as his major educational objectives. These are also, frequently, the type of behaviors which can be assessed most validly through observational tests.

The major function of an observational test is to increase the reliability of observation. Unguided observation can be very haphazard. We may see only portions of the behavior we are looking for, and the portion we see today may not be the same as the portion we see tomorrow. The conditions under which the performance occurs may vary from time to time. We may concentrate more on certain aspects of the performance at one time than at another time. These and similar weaknesses contribute to the low reliability of unaided observation. Observational tests aid the teacher by forcing him to observe under more tightly controlled conditions. This will inevitably increase the precision of his observations.

Observational tests have the natural advantage of relevance. In using such devices, the teacher is frequently observing procedures or products that are very similar to the ultimate objectives of his instruction. The speech teacher, for example, can be fairly well assured that the boy who speaks well in front of the class will also speak well when he addresses the PTA a few years hence. The social studies teacher, on the other hand, may have no real assurance that the girl who can write a dispassionate analysis of the causes of World War II will be able to use her ability as a future citizen to help avoid World War III.

The observational test, then, is typically high in relevance when used to assess those types of achievement for which it is naturally suited. On the other hand, the reliability of most such tests does not compare favorably with the reliability of the usual paper-and-pencil test. Since we like to have both reliability and relevance as high as we can, we opt for the observational test only in those areas where the paper-and-pencil test is clearly inappropriate.

There are four basic types of observational tests that are usually included in any discussion of this approach to educational assessment. These are (1) the anecdotal record, (2) the check list, (3) the rating scale, and (4) the participation chart. We shall discuss each type in that order.

ANECDOTAL RECORDS

The anecdotal record is the least structured of the techniques we will consider. As it is usually employed, the teacher simply describes in the form of an anecdote some behavior which he has observed and judged to be significant. The anecdote may be written on a plain piece of paper or on a special form which has been prepared for that purpose. It should be an objective description of the specific behavior either without interpretation or with the interpretation definitely separated from the description. The record is filed in a folder for the pupil. If more than one student is involved in an incident, separate records are prepared for each student.

Those teachers who wish to design their own anecdotal record forms should consider the inclusion of the following items:

1. A place for the name of the student.
2. A place for the date.
3. A small space for a description of the setting in which the incident occurred.
4. A relatively large space for a description of the incident.
5. A somewhat smaller space for an interpretation of the incident and for possible recommendations.
6. A place for the signature of the observer.

For many teachers, the most difficult aspect of the proper use of anecdotal records is maintaining objectivity in the description of the event. This is especially true when problem behavior is being described. There is a tendency to report such behavior using value-laden words such as "mean," "bad," or "nasty." The use of such words, however, introduces a confounding effect. The causes of the behavior, or rather the teacher's interpretation of the causes of behavior, are confused with the description of what occurred. An anecdotal record then might read: "John was a bad boy today. He picked a fight with Bill." The valued aspect of the first sentence is reasonably obvious and relatively easy to avoid. That of the second sentence is less obvious, but it must be recognized that saying John "picked" a fight is an interpretation of the behavior which occurred. John may have called Bill a name, or he may have struck Bill. The anecdotal record should state specifically what happened. Maintaining objectivity may be especially difficult in those situations when the teacher is directly involved. Consider, for example, the case where John is "sassy" or "rude" to the teacher. We may find that an objective description of what John did or said fails to convey the rudeness. We may explain this by saying: "It's not what he said; it's the way that he said it." This may well be true; sarcasm is frequently conveyed in the tone of voice. Nevertheless, valued terms like "sassy" and "rude" should be avoided in the description of the event.

If they are reported at all, they should be recognized as interpretations and relegated to the section of the report reserved for that purpose.

Note that the anecdotal record provides a systematic procedure for recording observations. It does not guarantee that those observations will be systematically made nor that they will be directed toward specific, relevant behaviors. For certain purposes these very points may be cited as advantages. If the teacher's attention is concentrated systematically on certain students and on looking for specific behaviors, there is a danger that he may miss other, significant behavior which he has not anticipated. On the other hand, if the teacher has not considered in advance specific behaviors which define the characteristics he is trying to assess, he may miss significant events which fail to attract his attention. In the area of personal adjustment, symptoms of withdrawal may well fall in this class. In any case, the control of what is reported is left in the hands of the teacher. Since it is simply a method of recording observations, there is no reason the anecdotal approach cannot be used in both structured and unstructured situations.

One procedure for introducing a system in making observations is *time sampling*. Under this procedure time is set aside specifically for observation. This time is divided among the various students, and the teacher concentrates on a scheduled individual for a relatively short period. Under this system, if fifteen minutes were allowed for concentrated observation of one pupil, it would of course be better to divide this into three five-minute blocks in order to allow temporary factors to vary. It seems quite reasonable that the teacher might use anecdotal records in summarizing the observations he has made through time sampling.

By exercising ingenuity, the classroom teacher can adapt the anecdotal record for use in assessing other aspects of academic achievement. This is particularly true in the elementary school, where the teacher is in more intimate contact with students for a longer period of time. It might be helpful to record, for example, an incident which demonstrated a given student's difficulty with a certain type of problem with a suggestion as to how this difficulty might be overcome. Since teachers' memories are as fallible as those of other professionally trained persons, such aids to future conduct might prove very beneficial.

The type of recording used in what is sometimes referred to as *precision teaching* can be considered a form of anecdotal record. It differs from the usual anecdotal record in the stress placed upon objectivity of observation and recording. In brief, precision teaching requires that some complete cycle of behavior be identified for purposes of observation. For example, rising and leaving one's seat during class time would be such an identifiable cycle of behavior. Using time sampling procedures, a teacher records the number of completed cycles per unit of time to establish the rate of the behavior. This initial rate is called the *baseline* rate of the behavior. Then the teacher initiates procedures designed to alter the rate of the behavior either up or down. Subsequent observations conducted in the same fashion will help determine if the rate of the behavior has indeed been altered. A more complete description of this process can be found in the book by Meacham and Wiesen.[1]

THE CHECK LIST

At this point, it is probably well to define exactly what we mean by check lists and rating scales. A *check list* is an instrument consisting of a list of behaviors or characteristics whose presence or absence is to be determined when observing a performance or product. Normally, a check is placed in an appropriate spot on the paper if observation confirms the presence of the behavior or characteristic sought—hence the name "check list." Here, in Fig. 4.1, is an example:

[1] Merle L. Meacham and Allen E. Wiesen, *Changing Classroom Behavior* (Pennsylvania's International Textbook Co., Scranton, Pa., 1969).

Figure 4.1 Check list for teacher demonstrations in industrial arts.

Behaviors	Yes	No
1. All necessary tools and equipment on hand.	————	————
2. Necessary tools and equipment properly arranged.	————	————
3. Instructor talked to class, not to tools, etc.	————	————
4. Instructor demonstrated only one operation at a time.	————	————
5. Etc.		

THE RATING SCALE

A *rating scale*, on the other hand, goes beyond recording merely the presence or absence of certain behaviors. It places the behavior at some point along a continuum and provides the opportunity to note qualitative differences in performance. Consider the following example in Fig. 4.2:

Figure 4.2 Rating scale for compositions.

I. Paragraph construction		
0	5	10
No sign of unity. Paper incoherent.	Some attempt to unify ideas.	Paragraph shows a unified and coherent plan.
II. Sentence construction		
0	5	10
Sentences all relatively short. No variety in sentence patterns. Majority are simple sentences.	Varied length of sentences. Attempts made to use different patterns. About half are simple sentences.	Used great variety in sentence length and pattern. No more than ¼ are simple sentences.
III. Etc.		

There is a certain amount of variation in both check lists and rating scales. Check lists sometimes use three categories rather than two. Instead of checking simply "yes" or "no," an intermediate category of "sometimes" could be used. When this occurs, however, the check list begins to blend into the rating scale, because a continuum rather than a dichotomy of observation is being established.

Numerical rating scale. There are three basic types of rating scales: (1) the *numerical* rating scale, (2) the *graphic* rating scale, and (3) the *descriptive graphic* rating scale. Of the three, the numerical rating scale

Figure 4.3 Guide for evaluating research papers.

Name of student _____ Date _____

Rating scale
5 4 3 2 1

I. Problem
Rating for clearness of statement, conciseness,
limitation of problem, etc.

II. Method
A. Rating for statement of method
B. Rating for research ability indicated

III. The Literature
Rating for adequacy of the review and the
command of sources

IV. Treatment and presentation of results
Rating for research ability indicated

V. Mechanical organization
A. Features (check presence—one point for each)
1. Preface
2. Table of contents
3. List of tables
4. List of figures
5. Bibliography
B. Rating for organization of tables
C. Rating for organization of figures
D. Rating for form of citations and bibliography

VI. English
Rating for spelling, punctuation, diction, etc.

Score
Grade

is the simplest. It consists of a list of behaviors, traits, or features which are to be observed, together with a fixed numerical scale against which they are to be judged. In most cases, the scale includes the numbers 1, 2, 3, 4, and 5. Figure 4.3 gives an example of a numerical rating scale. The numerical rating scale is probably least reliable of the three types because of lack of agreement concerning the meaning of the numerical values on the scale. Where such meaning can be established through familiarity with the scale, however, it does provide a simple and direct approach to assessment.

Graphic rating scale. The graphic rating scale differs from the numerical rating scale in two ways. First, it uses words rather than numbers to indicate points along the scale; second, it employs a line to indicate the continuum for the trait or behavior to be observed with the understand-

Figure 4.4 Scale for evaluating performance on a brass instrument.

Name _____ Date _____

Directions: Place a check mark at the appropriate place on each scale to indicate how the student's performance compares with expected performance for sixth-grade children.

1. Posture

Below average	Average	Above average

2. Holding of instrument

Below average	Average	Above average

3. Embouchure placement

Below average	Average	Above average

4. Breath control and support

Below average	Average	Above average

5. Fingering

Below average	Average	Above average

6. Instrument care

Below average	Average	Above average

ing that the individual may fall at any point along this continuum. Figure 4.4 gives an example of a graphic rating scale.

The scale shown in Fig. 4.4 is known as a *constant-alternatives* type of scale because the descriptive words employed remain the same for all traits or behaviors to be observed. Another type, known as the *changing-alternatives* type, may employ different descriptive words for each trait or behavior if this seems appropriate.

The graphic rating scale does have the advantage of providing a continuum so the individual may be placed at any point along the scale. This may be only an apparent advantage, however, since it is likely that an observer can make finer discriminations than those represented by the five different categories.

Moreover, the use of words rather than numbers probably does not do much to increase the reliability of the scale. It is probably as difficult to agree upon the meaning of "average" as it is to agree upon the meaning of "3" on a scale of five points.

Descriptive graphic rating scale. The descriptive graphic rating scale is similar to the graphic rating scale, except that instead of using one or two words to indicate the points on the scale, it uses a more elaborate description of the behavior or trait to be observed. The advantage of this approach is that it enables the observer to compare the performance he sees with a description of typical performance at any point along the scale. Presumably, this allows him to make a more accurate placement of the observed behavior. Because of this increased precision, the descriptive graphic rating scale tends to be more reliable than the other two types. Figure 4.5 gives an example of a descriptive graphic rating scale.

DEVELOPING CHECK LISTS AND RATING SCALES

The first step in developing a check list or a rating scale is to state your instructional objectives. The behavioral approach to stating ob-

ᵍure 4.5   Scale for evaluating proposed room adjustments in home economics.

Function 1	Name 3	5
ttle evidence that e needs of the family re considered.	Evidence of consideration of family needs. Traffic patterns considered.	Excellent evaluation of the needs of family. Traffic patterns are well thought out, as well as window spaces, and other points of emphasis.

Color 1	3	5
ttle evidence of thought color and its dramatic fects.	Color scheme included but there is need to show general areas of color in the room.	An excellent illustration on areas of color; appears to be a livable color scheme— variety in color.

. Lighting 1	3	5
ttle evidence of thought useful and decorative rposes of lighting.	A good arrangement of lighting effects, including both general and area lighting.	Creative and functional use of lighting.

. Window Treatments 1	3	5
ttle evidence of thought ven to window treatment. lor and style not clear.	Ordinary treatment of window space.	Creative window treatment and good illustration of desired effect (type of fabric which would go well in room.)

Elements of Design 1	3	5
ttle thought to design ements. Room appears balanced, has no parent rhythm and is t to scale.	The room appears balanced. Some application of rhythm principle. Room has some unity.	Excellent balance of room; all parts of the room work together. The rhythm gives unity to the room.

Score_____

Grade_____

Note that the scale in Fig. 4.5 uses numbers along the top of the line representing the continuum so a score can be derived for the project.

jectives is particularly well suited to check lists and rating scales, because once the behaviors are specified, they can be translated almost directly into the corpus of a measuring instrument. Perhaps this can best be illustrated with an example.

A high school teacher of English wished to develop an instrument suitable for measuring the outcome of instruction on a unit on poetry. He wanted to measure something other than the usual ability to pair poet and poem or to recognize instances of simile and metaphor. He wanted to see whether he could impart something of the poet's craft to his tenth graders. How could he tell whether he had succeeded? He began by writing four objectives for the unit. These objectives specified the behavior the students ought to be able to exhibit at the conclusion of the unit. These were his objectives:

1. Without the aid of class notes or textbook and working at home, the student ought to be able to compose a simple two-stanza, eight-line poem of the metric pattern iambic pentameter with errors in no more than two of the eight lines.

2. Under the same conditions, he ought to be able to compose a simple three-stanza, nine-line poem employing his choice of the following metric patterns: (a) trochaic, (b) anapestic, or (c) dactylic. The poem should contain no more than three metric feet in any line and should contain errors in no more than three of the nine lines.

3. The student also ought to be able to compose during class time one each of the following stanzaic forms: (a) heroic couplet, (b) quatrain, and (c) tercet. All should be free from errors in length, rhyme, and number of metric feet, where applicable.

4. The student also ought to be able to compose during class times three examples each of simile and metaphor. All examples should show clear differentiation between these two poetic devices by the inclusion (where applicable) or exclusion of the words "like" or "as."

Having written these objectives, he decided that a simple check list would suffice for assessing whether the students had achieved the objectives. In this case, he would analyze the product, not the process. The product would be the poetry and the portions of poetry the students had written. The check list he produced is presented in Fig. 4.6. The results from this check list could be used either for grading or for diagnosing what the students had or had not learned during the unit.

Let us show how another teacher went about developing a rating scale for use in her class. This teacher was attempting to teach the rudiments of laboratory procedure to a fourth-grade class during the course of a unit on magnetism. She was also interested in getting her class to work cooperatively during the laboratory experience. This is the way she set up her objectives:

Figure 4.6 Check list for assignment on mechanics of poetry.

Name _____ Date _____

DIRECTIONS: Check "Yes" or "No" as appropriate

	Yes	No
1. (a) Does the first poem contain two four-line stanzas?		
(b) Do six of the eight lines have iambic stress?		
(c) Do six of the eight lines contain pentameter?		
2. (a) Is the second poem trochaic, dactylic, or anapestic (one of the three)?		
(b) Does the poem contain three three-line stanzas?		
(c) Does the poem contain more than three metric feet in any line?		
3. (a) Does the heroic couplet contain two lines of iambic pentameter with end rhyme?		
(b) Does the quatrain contain four lines rhymed in any manner?		
(c) Does the tercet contain three lines with a single rhyme?		
4. (a) Do all similes compare by use of "like" or "as"?		
(b) Do all metaphors make implied comparisons without using the words "like" or "as"?		

Given the opportunity to work in small laboratory groups on a scientific study of magnetism, the students should be able to:

1. Follow the instruction of the laboratory supervisor without requesting further help.

2. Be cautious with all laboratory equipment.

3. Begin work promptly.

4. Record data carefully and accurately.

5. Transfer data to a table or graph.

6. Communicate verbally about observations, inferences, and conclusions drawn from data.

7. Do his fair share of the work during laboratory time.

8. Clean and return equipment to its proper place at the end of the laboratory period.

Having written these objectives, she devised the rating sheet shown in Fig. 4.7.

Again the use of such a rating scale would allow the teacher to obtain a score for grading or to use the results for diagnosing individual strengths and weaknesses in achievement.

USES OF CHECK LISTS AND RATING SCALES

We have already discussed in general some of the uses of check lists and rating scales, but examples of more specific applications might be helpful.

Measurement. Both check lists and rating scales can be used to provide measures on achievement variables. In the case of the check list, this must, of necessity, be a relatively crude measure. About all that can be done is to count the number of checks of a positive nature and rank students in order of this count. This procedure will produce ordinal data of a low level of refinement.

Rating scales (despite the implication of the name) also produce only ordinal data. The data from rating scales fit our definition of measurement more closely, however, since they do postulate a series of continuous variables and provide schemes for classifying such variables.

Figure 4.7 Scientific laboratory rating sheet.

Date _____

Student's name _____

DIRECTIONS: To the lab instructor—Make your ratings on each of the following characteristics by placing an X anywhere along the horizontal line under each question. In the space for comments include anything helpful to clarify your rating.

Score

1. To what extent does the pupil follow instructions? ___

1	2	3	4	5	6	7	8	9	10
needs excessive help				sometimes needs help				needs no extra help	

2. To what extent does the pupil care for the equipment? ___

1	2	3	4	5	6	7	8	9	10
unduly careless				usually careful				cautious	

3. To what extent does student begin work promptly? ___

1	2	3	4	5	6	7	8	9	10
needs prompting				slow but steady				begins promptly	

4. Does student record data carefully and accurately? ___

1	2	3	4	5	6	7	8	9	10
careless and obscure				better than average				records carefully	

5. Does student transfer data accurately to tables and graphs? ___

10	9	8	7	6	5	4	3	2	1
neat and accurate				fair				sloppy and careless	

6. To what extent does student communicate verbally about discoveries? ___

10	9	8	7	6	5	4	3	2	1
all the time				frequently				never	

7. Does student do his share during experiments and cleaning? ___

10	9	8	7	6	5	4	3	2	1
always				usually				never	

COMMENTS: _____

_____

Hence, we are more likely to regard results from rating scales than from check lists to represent "true" measures.

Process analysis. There are many areas of the curriculum in the typical school where the activities and skills which are taught are really not amenable to measurement with paper-and-pencil tests. It is in such areas where the observational test is most useful. Here are some examples:

1. Physical education—The so-called *skills* tests qualify as observational tests. The teacher is interested in how well the student can perform certain skills or how well he can play certain games. The only way to do this is to use some form of controlled observation.

2. Speech—The prime test of instruction in speech is speaking. A student may know very well what it is that he is supposed to do in order to give a good speech, but he may fail miserably when he gets in front of a group.

3. Science—One of the outcomes of instruction in science is the ability to manipulate laboratory equipment properly. Such ability can be assessed by means of a checklist or rating scale.

4. Music—One of the most difficult areas in which to obtain valid measurement is music. As a consequence, most music teachers give up the whole attempt as a bad job and assign all A's and B's to their students because they really have no good measures of achievement. With some thought, however, a music teacher should be able to identify the behaviors which constitute musicianship and devise a rating scale to measure such behaviors.

There are many other areas of performance which could be mentioned, but these will serve as examples.

Product analysis. In many cases, it is the product, not the process, which we wish to measure. Here are examples of such products:

1. Home economics—In teaching sewing, we are interested in the quality of dress a girl can produce. Or we may be interested in the cakes she bakes or the color schemes she produces for a living room. All these are products and their quality can be assessed by means of a rating scale or a check list.

2. Industrial arts—Here, too, the student produces certain products made of wood or metal. The teacher normally has specifications for such products, and these specifications can serve as the basis for the construction of a check list or rating scale designed to assess the quality of the product.

3. Art—The field of art is another area where precise measurement is very difficult. Some would claim that it is impossible. However, there must be certain criteria which differentiate a quality art product from an inferior product. If these criteria can be specified, they can be incorporated into a check list or rating scale.

4. English—We may not normally think of the essay as a product, but it is. It is the product of the writer's creative thought. As a product, its quality may be more reliably assessed with the aid of some systematic aid to observation rather than by the more holistic approach employed by most teachers of English.

It is obvious that in certain areas, both process and product are important. In sewing, for example, we wish the student not only to produce a quality dress but also to use the appropriate techniques in producing the dress. In such cases, our rating scales or check lists can include elements representing both process and product.

Diagnosis. In many situations, we are really not concerned about obtaining a measure of achievement. We are rather concerned about strengths and weaknesses in performance so we may use such information for instructional purposes. This is the process of diagnosis, and observational tests serve a very useful function here. Both teacher and student can view the results from a check list or rating scale and know what has to be done to improve performance.

PARTICIPATION CHARTS

Participation charts are similar to check lists in that in using such a device the teacher simply records the presence or absence of a certain behavior. They differ from check lists principally in that they are used to record the performance of a number of students at the same time. As the name implies, participation charts are used to record the participation of students in certain activities in which participation is itself an objective of instruction. One such activity, for example, is group discussion where one objective well might be that each student will take an active part.

There are two common formats for participation charts. One consists of a sheet of paper which has been ruled into rows and columns. The names of the pupils in the class are entered in each row, and the observations are recorded in the columns. The use of the rows and columns, of course, could be reversed. The other format consists of a chart like a seating diagram. Cells on the chart are arranged to correspond to the seating in the room. Observations are recorded in these cells with the advantage that the observer need not be familiar with the names of the students. In either format and in the simplest use, the observer simply tallies the number of times each student participates.

It is frequently desirable to elaborate the recording scheme to operate as a rating scale. A disadvantage of a simple tally of frequency of contribution is that it makes no distinctions regarding the quality of the remark. A simple "Uh huh" rates as equivalent to the expression of a trenchant insight. To gain precision the observer can use some system to indicate the quality of the contribution as well as the fact of participation. A frequently employed scheme uses four categories:

1. A major contribution, which would be a remark which introduced a new and relevant idea or one which produced some clarification or insight into an idea under discussion.

2. A minor contribution, which would be a remark which supplied a new example to illustrate an idea or which served to keep the discussion moving toward clarification of ideas already presented.

3. A neutral contribution, which would be an indication of assent to a question or a statement of doubtful value which was, nevertheless, on the topic.

4. A negative contribution, which would be the introduction of an idea which is irrelevant to the discussion or the employment of caustic remarks which promote disharmony within the group.

These various degrees of quality can be indicated on the participation chart by a number or symbol code; for example 2, 1, 0, and -1, or #, +, 0, -. The number code can be used as weights and a crude index of performance derived by summing the entries for each student. The system suggested here implies that a neutral contribution is no better than no contribution at all. If the teacher does not agree with this assumption, different weights can be assigned. The results of this more refined analysis can be useful both in helping students analyze their own performance and in assigning grades on the basis of their participation.

SUGGESTIONS FOR THE USE OF OBSERVATIONAL TESTS

There are a number of suggestions which can be made concerning the use of observational tests.

1. Do not use them as substitutes for paper-and-pencil tests. As we pointed out earlier in this chapter, the major advantage of the observational test is its inherent relevance for those situations in which the paper-and-pencil test is inappropriate. However, the observational test is normally less reliable than the paper-and-pencil test under almost any conditions. Use observational tests, then, only in situations where they are clearly more relevant than a paper-and-pencil test.

2. Experiment with preliminary forms of check lists and rating scales. Reproduce only a small number to begin with and try these out. What you will frequently find is that revisions need to be made. You are more likely to make such revisions if you do not have 200 copies on hand which you feel compelled to use.

3. When using observational tests, record quickly. It is best, of course, if you can record immediately as you view the performance or the product. If this cannot be done, do your recording as soon as possible after the observation. The human memory is fallible, and any extensive delay in recording increases the unreliability of the results.

4. Guard against the *halo effect* in using rating scales. The halo effect is the tendency to let our general impression of a person or a product influence all of our ratings. If our impression is favorable, all ratings tend to be high; if it is unfavorable, they tend to be low. Obviously, few performances or products are uniformly excellent or incompetent. Since one of the major features of a rating scale is the diagnostic information it provides, due care should be given to the independence of the rating of every trait or behavior measured by the scale.

5. Use a number of raters to increase reliability. In a team teaching situation, all the teachers can rate all the students. Where there is only one teacher, students may serve as raters. Students from the upper elementary grades on can be trained as raters. This serves at least two functions. It helps the teacher by providing independent ratings that can be used in making evaluations. It also helps the students by making them more sensitive observers and, perhaps, better judges of their own performance.

6. Be cautious in deriving a "total" score from rating scales. Normally we weight the various traits to be measured by their importance to the overall performance or product. There are some situations, however, where a score of zero on one of the traits is sufficient to vitiate the entire performance. There is an apocryphal story about a group of 4-H boys that illustrates this point. It seems that their adult leader was instructing them in the art of judging cattle using a rating scale he had prepared. Their "final exam" was to take place at the county fair in the cattle barns. At that time the leader called all of the boys together, explaining that he had chosen at random for each of them a bull from the list of registered entries. Each boy was to find his bull, rate it, and return the rating sheet to the leader. The leader would then go to the

barns, rate the bulls himself, and compare his ratings with the ones submitted by the boys. Everything was going nicely until he came to the rating sheet submitted by Johnny. Johnny had rated his bull as absolutely tops in all categories except one. This was the category labeled "vitality." The leader wondered how such an apparently fine animal could be so low in this particular respect, so he asked Johnny to lead him to the bull. Johnny led him through the barn to the outside where he pointed to the bull. There he was—a truly magnificent creature. He had only one major weakness. He was dead!

5
PAPER-AND-PENCIL TESTS

Although observational tests deserve to be more widely employed in assessing the outcomes of school instruction, it will likely be some time before their popularity challenges that of paper-and-pencil tests. This type of test, in its manifold forms, has been with us for hundreds, perhaps thousands, of years. When we think of achievement testing, it is the type of test we think of first. Perhaps this is because of its more formal nature and its closer associations with success or failure in the classroom. Since it is undoubtedly the most important assessment device in current use in the schools, we need to spend a good deal of our time telling how it should most properly be used.

THE TABLE OF SPECIFICATIONS

Any good classroom test should begin with preplanning. This is most often not the case. The construction of a classroom test is one of those things frequently put off until the last minute. In a great rush we slap together a few true-false items or scribble down a couple of essay items and congratulate ourselves that we have beaten the deadline. But as in most of life's other activities, last-minute efforts are frequently inadequate efforts. To do a competent job of constructing a classroom test, we must lay our plans before we begin. This preplanning for testing is facilitated by the creation of a *table of specifications,* sometimes called a *test blueprint.*

The table of specifications is essentially a two-way classification of the items which will constitute the test we propose to write. One classification is the content to be covered by the test; the other classification is the objectives to be measured. In the cells of the table formed by the two-way classification scheme, we place either numbers or percentages. If numbers, the number stands for the number of items so classified which will be included in the test. If percentages, the percentage is that proportion of the total number of items in the test to be allotted to the cell. Figure 5.1 gives an example of such a table prepared for a fifth-grade test on sound. Note that the elements of content to be covered are listed on the left-hand side and the objectives are listed across the top. This arrangement could be reversed if it proves to be more convenient to do so.

Figure 5.1 Table of specifications for test on sound.

	Objectives					
	Knows	Knows	Understands	Applies	Interprets	
Content	Common Terms	Specific Facts	General Principles	General Principles	Charts and Graphs	Totals
Importance of sound	—	—	4	3	—	7
Elements needed for sound	1	1	4	2	—	8
Sound waves	1	1	1	1	—	4
Differences in sounds	1	3	3	1	2	10
Parts of the ear	5	1	—	—	2	8
Sound and the ear	—	—	4	1	—	5
Hearing loss	1	2	—	—	—	3
	9	8	16	8	4	45

As we discussed in the chapter on objectives, the objectives for a classroom test are most often unobservable or cognitive behaviors. Consequently, in most blueprints for classroom tests you will find statements such as "knowledge of specific facts," "the ability to apply principles to novel situations," or "the ability to draw valid inferences from data." There is no complete agreement on the method of wording or the types of such cognitive behaviors, nor need there be. They may vary from one-word descriptions such as "Identifying" to more elaborate and specific statements such as "The ability to predict outcomes under specified conditions." The teacher must suit himself in this respect and employ whatever terminology seems most appropriate for his purposes.

The basic purpose of a blueprint is to increase the relevance of the test. The blueprint helps to do this by ensuring that the test is "balanced," that is, ensuring that no important outcome or element of content has been overlooked in its construction. It is all too easy for a teacher to write test items predominately for those content areas which either he finds most personally appealing or in which he finds it easiest to create item ideas. When this occurs, students rightfully complain that the test was not "fair," because, judging from their perceptions of class discussion and readings, the test did not adequately cover the appropriate material.

Balance is achieved by appropriate assigning of weights within the blueprint. As we pointed out before, these weights refer either to the number of items which will be devoted to each category or the percentage of the total number of items which will be so assigned. For classroom tests, it is simpler and easier to use merely the number of items. The decision as to the number of items to be assigned to each cell in the blueprint depends essentially upon two things: (a) the relative importance of this objective or this element of content and (b) the emphasis given to it in class. Normally, both these criteria should be employed in assigning weights.

A certain complication in assigning weights occurs in the case of essay items. Where objectively scored items only are to be employed, the matter is simple—one item, one unit of weight. If part of the test is to consist of essay items, however, then the weight should reflect the total number of points which will be allotted to those items.

Not all cells will have weights listed for them. This simply reflects the fact that this particular objective is not relevant to this particular area of content.

Certain bits of advice can be offered for the construction of test blueprints. First of all, it is probably better to begin with a more detailed specification of content than will eventually be used. As you draw up the blueprint in its rough form, you can see where categories can be combined with no great loss in precision. Second, the initial blueprint may not exactly correspond with the completed test. Even though you have specified a certain number of items for a given cell, you may find it impossible to produce all the items you have specified. In such a case, you have no alternative but to make changes in your design. Last, the weightings assigned by allocating certain numbers of items to certain outcomes may not give a completely accurate picture. Such a procedure assumes independence among items. If items are correlated, the outcomes measured by such items receive increased weight. This is a technical matter, however, which need not be of great concern to the classroom teacher.

ITEM FORMS

Once the table of specifications has been completed, the next task is to decide the type of item forms which will be most appropriate for assessing the outcomes specified. To some extent, the instructional objective is a controlling factor in the type of item form employed. If the objective specifies "knowledge," a variety of item forms might be used. If the objective specifies "application," however, the matter of item forms which can be used is somewhat narrowed.

In the following pages we propose to discuss the major item forms which are potentially useful to the classroom teacher. There are six of these: (1) the short-answer form, (2) the true-false form, (3) the multiple-choice form, (4) the matching form, (5) the classification form, and (6) the essay form. These six do not exhaust all the types of item forms, but they do represent those in most common use. If the teacher has command of these, he can meet the requirements of almost any type of paper-and-pencil test.

THE SHORT-ANSWER FORM

The *short-answer* form is the simplest of all the item forms. It is the well-known "fill-in-the-blanks" type of item. The examinee either responds to a direct question or he inserts words at appropriate places as directed. There are three basic varieties of the short-answer form. They are: (1) the *question* variety, (2) the *completion* variety, and (3) the *identification* or *association* variety.

The question variety. As the term implies, the question variety consists simply of a question to which the examinee supplies an answer. Here is an example:

1. What was the name of the ship that carried the Pilgrims to Plymouth Colony in 1620? _____

The completion variety. The completion variety is the familiar fill-in-the-blanks exercise. The examinee is presented with a sentence in which one or more words have been deleted. In their place is a blank. The task of the examinee is to supply the missing words. Here is an example:

2. The last names of the first three presidents of the U.S. were
_____, _____, and _____.

The association or identification variety. This variety is normally used as part of an exercise, that is, a number of items related to each other by some specified structure. The examinee is supplied with a word. He is then asked to supply another word associated with the first in some manner as specified in the directions to the exercise. Here is an example:

Directions: In the blank provided, write the last name of the man who was president of the U.S. at the time the given event occurred.

1. The War of 1812 _____
2. The Missouri Compromise _____
3. The Homestead Act _____
4. The Teapot Dome Scandal _____

Applicability of the short-answer form. It is readily apparent that the short-answer item form cannot be readily used to test much other than knowledge of specific facts. It simply does not lend itself to the testing of higher-order cognitive outcomes. It has a special appeal for many teachers, however, because it does measure recall rather than recognition. That is, the examinee is required to search his memory and *produce* a response. He is not allowed to *choose* a response from a set of alternatives. Whether the former is really a more useful type of achievement is, of course, a debatable matter.

Suggestions for writing short-answer items. Although the short-answer item is widely used by teachers in constructing classroom tests, and although it is a very simple type of item form, teachers do make mistakes in its construction. Here are some helpful suggestions to consider when writing such items:

1. Be sure that the item can be answered *only* by a *unique* word, phrase, or number. If it cannot, you may find yourself challenged by a student who insists that his answer to the question is as correct as your own. Take this item as an example:

Congress convenes in _____ .

Presumably the author of this item meant the answer to be "January." Disregarding the fact that it may also convene in other months, a student could write "emergencies" or "Washington, D. C." and present a good defense of his answer. The effect of this is to introduce a certain element of subjectivity into the scoring. Some answers may be considered correct. Other equally good answers may, for reasons best known to the teacher, be considered incorrect. When this occurs, the reliability of the test is lowered.

It should be noted that the use of the question variety eliminates some of the possibilities for multiple answers. In the example above, a question cannot be framed for which both time and place are appropriate answers. Minimally the question would have to be either "When does Congress convene?" or "Where does Congress convene?" Of course, both of these are still somewhat ambiguous. The first would be better stated, "In what month does the regular session of Congress convene?"

2. Provide as many spaces as there are words in the answer. The student may be confused if he sees only one blank when he knows there is more than one word to the answer. Here is an example:

The _____ _____ _____ occurred when a group of American revolutionaries disguised as Indians captured an English ship in the harbor at Boston and threw the cargo into the water.

3. It is frequently advisable to have the student write his answers in blanks placed either to the left or the right of the items rather than directly in the sentence itself. This will make it easier to score the items because the answers are grouped together in a convenient location instead of being strung out in random fashion in the middle of the page. Consider this example:

a. _____ The three nations currently leading the world
in the production of rubber latex are

b. _____ ___a___ , ___b___ , and ___c___ .

c. _____

Notice that in the example the blanks inside the sentence are made short and the letter referring to the blank at the left of the item is placed directly in the center of the blank in the sentence. This is to make it difficult for the student to misunderstand the directions and write his answer where he should not.

4. When using the completion variety, do not delete so many words that the student will find it difficult to determine the meaning of the sentence. Take this example:

The _____ of _____ is a _____ _____ of

_____.

In this case, no one but the person who wrote the item would know what went into the blanks.

THE TRUE-FALSE FORM

The *true-false item form* is one of the most widely used of all types of items. Some would say, however, that it is also the most widely misused. At the surface level, it appears a relatively simple form, easy to construct and use. It consists merely of a declarative statement containing an assertion which the student is to judge true or false. This apparent simplicity is deceptive, however, because the true-false item is, in reality, one of the most difficult types of items to write properly. There are two major reasons for this.

First, outside the realms of formal knowledge (e.g., mathematics, grammar, logic) there are few assertions or propositions which can be judged unambiguously true or false. Most of the major truths in other fields come in shades of gray, and even experts are prone to attach probability figures to their assertions. This often means that such major truths are not fit fodder for true-false items. Instead we must often restrict ourselves to more minor truths.

Second, the true-false item is more prone to ambiguity than most other item forms. Outside of love letters, there are probably few types of writing that are read more intensively than test items. A single word, loosely employed, can throw terror into the heart of an examinee. In a multiple-choice item, he can use the responses to aid in interpreting the question. In the true-false item, however, the statement stands alone. It must be sufficient unto itself, and if it is not, the author can rightfully be charged with introducing unnecessary ambiguity.

There are a number of variations of the true-false form, all of which can be subsumed under the more general heading of *alternate-response* items. We shall discuss some of the more useful of such varieties.

Basic variety. The basic variety is simply a declarative sentence containing an assertion or proposition which the student is to judge as true or false. Here is an example of the way in which it is more commonly written:

T F 1. Plymouth Colony was founded in 1620.

The correction variety. In the correction variety of true-false items, the student is to do two things. First, he is to judge whether the statement is true or false, just as in the basic variety. Next, however, if the statement is false, he is to write whatever words are necessary to convert it to a true statement. The truth or falsity of the statement always depends upon a certain critical portion which is underlined. It is the underlined word or words which the student must replace if the statement is to be made true. Here is an example:

T F 2. <u>Jefferson</u> was the first president of the United States.

This variety of true-false item appeals to many teachers because it combines recall with recognition. If the student recognizes the falsity of the statement, he must recall the word or words necessary to correct it.

There are two things the teacher should be aware of when using this variety. First, it is essential that a key portion of the statement be underlined. Chaos can occur if it is not. In the simple example of the item given above, for example, the student might have written "third" in the blank if "Jefferson" had not been underlined. Had it been a lengthier and more complicated statement, even more possibilities would have been opened up.

Second, be careful when you score such items. Remember that there are really two scoring units for such an item, one of which is essentially a form of short answer. If the statement is true and the student marks it true, he gets two points. If it is false and if he marks it false and corrects it properly, he also gets two points. If it is false and he marks it false but fails to correct it properly he gets one point. Of course, if it is false and he marks it true or true and he marks it false, he gets no points. This scoring is not terribly complicated, but unless the teacher is alert, he may make clerical errors. Certainly this variety is more difficult to score than the basic variety of true-false.

Any type of phenomenon which can be cast into a true dichotomy can be used for alternate-response items. Here are some additional examples:

Right-wrong variety. In such items, the student is to judge the statement right or wrong rather than true or false. One common application is in the field of English where a student is given a sentence and asked to decide whether it is correctly or incorrectly stated. If there are no errors of any sort, he is to mark it "right." If there are any errors of any sort, he is to mark it "wrong." Here is an example:

R W   3. Running downhill, the ball fell between my legs and tripped me.

More-less variety. This variety is frequently used to test the student's knowledge of relative magnitude. He is given two magnitudes. If the one on the left is greater than the one on the right, he is to mark "more"; if it is smaller he is to mark "less." Here are two examples:

More Less 4. 1/8 0.13

More Less 5. $\sqrt{0.29}$ 0.47

Fact-opinion variety. This variety is used to test whether students can discriminate between that which could reasonably be regarded as a statement of fact and that which is more likely to be a statement of opinion. Here are three examples:

F O 6. While still on board the Mayflower, the Pilgrims drew up a "compact" to form the basis for the government of the colony.

F O 7. Because of the severity of the first winter, some of the Pilgrims expressed a desire to return to England.

F O 8. The form of government of Plymouth Colony was superior to that of Virginia Colony.

CONFIDENCE WEIGHTING

One of the criticisms leveled against the true-false item is that it offers little diagnostic information to the teacher. If a student misses an item, you cannot be sure whether he simply guessed and lost or whether he carefully weighed relevant pieces of information and came to the wrong conclusions. One device which has been suggested as a partial antidote to this weakness is the *confidence-weighting* approach.

Confidence weighting is basically a different method of scoring the true-false item. It combines some of the elements of the classification form, to be discussed later in this chapter, with the true-false form. In addition, it provides for differential scoring of responses.

Confidence weighting is normally used with an *exercise*, that is, a situation where a number of items having some functional unity are employed. Appropriate instructions are given to the student and then he is told that his answers will be scored in the following manner:

Response number	Level of confidence of this response	Right	Score value Wrong	Omit
1.	I am certain this statement is true.	2	-2	
2.	I believe the statement to be true, but I am not certain.	1	0	
3.	I do not know whether this statement is true or false.			1/2
4.	I believe the statement to be false, but I am not certain.	1	0	
5.	I am certain this statement is false.	2	-2	

The teacher should be aware that in using a confidence-weighting approach, he is in reality measuring two things. First, he is measuring the student's knowledge about the subject, and second, the state of the student's awareness of the level of his knowledge. The latter can likely be considered to be a relevant outcome of instruction.

Obviously, the major disadvantage of the confidence-weighting scheme is the complexity of the scoring procedure. When scoring by hand, the teacher must assign the proper weight to each student response and then sum these weights. There is much more chance for clerical error in this process than if each response is merely given a weight of 1 if correct and 0 if incorrect. It may be open to question, in the absence of mechanical aids, whether the additional information obtained justifies the increased complexity of the scoring procedure.

SUGGESTIONS FOR WRITING TRUE-FALSE ITEMS

The true-false item is one of the most difficult item forms to write well. Improved items will result, however, if a number of precautions are taken. These are some of the most important:

1. Do not make your items too long. The major reason for this

admonition is that excessive length introduces the irrelevant factor of reading into the item. This is especially true if the added length is due to qualifying words and phrases which the item writer feels are necessary to produce a true statement. In addition to the added burden of reading, with the attendant possibility of ambiguity which this produces, the extra length may provide an irrelevant clue because inexperienced item writers tend to make true statements longer than false statements.

2. Avoid irrelevant clues provided by *specific determiners*. A specific determiner is a key word which allows the students to guess the correct answer on the basis of test sophistication when he really does not know the answer. For example, statements which contain the key words "all," "none," "never," "always," "only," or "no" are usually false. Conversely, statements which contain the words "generally," "frequently," "sometimes," "could," "might," or "may" are usually true.

It is sometimes permissible to take advantage of the tendency of students to use such clues when they do not know the answers if you can use the clue in the reverse way. Take this item, for example:

T F   The sum of the deviations of a set of raw scores from their mean will always equal zero.

If the student responded to the "always" without knowing the answer, he would miss the item.

3. Avoid irrelevant clues provided by undue specificity in the item. Such statements usually tend to be true. Here is an example:

T F   Twenty-seven nations eventually entered World War I.

4. Avoid negatively worded items. Above all, avoid negatively worded false items. Consider this example:

T F   Knowledge of results does not have a facilitating effect on learning.

Note that in a straightforward form, i.e., "Knowledge of results has a facilitating effect on learning," it would be a relatively easy item. Worded in a negative fashion, it becomes very puzzling, and even the student who possesses the requisite information might find it difficult to answer.

5. Avoid items containing listings of things some of which may be true and some of which may be false. Take this example from a fourth-grade test:

T F   Sound travels through air, liquids, solids, and vacuums.

6. Test only one point in each item. Particularly, do not have two points, one of which is true and the other false. Here is an example:

T F   Pacific Ocean salmon ascend fresh water rivers to spawn
        and then descend again to the ocean.

When such items are keyed "false," there is always the possibility the student may receive credit for erroneous information. Consider this item, for example:

T F   George Washington was first inaugurated President of the
        U. S. in Philadelphia on April 30, 1789.

The statement is false since the inauguration was held in New York. Suppose, however, that a student thinks that Philadelphia is correct but that the year was 1791 or that the date was other than April 30. This student, too, will mark the item "false" and will receive credit for the wrong reason.

7. Do not use statements of opinion as the basis for items unless you attribute the opinion to the source.

T F   According to Franklin D. Roosevelt, a balanced budget
        should be the backbone of the national economy.

Note that the item in this form really tests whether the student knows the views of the person or the organization in question. If the item were merely a question of opinion without the attribution, it would be improper as a true-false item.

8. Do not "lift" statements from a textbook and expect them to function well as true-false items. In the first place, this practice reinforces the tendency toward rote learning of textual material. In the second place, such statements tend to be true more often than false, and the student may use the stereotyped language as a clue. Take the following example:

T F Feelings ran high in England as a consequence of the
       Boston Tea Party.

9. Do not use "trick" items where an apparently true statement is rendered false by an insignificant detail. Take the following example:

T F The area of a rectangle 4 ft. by 3 ft. is equal to 12 sq. yds.

10. Avoid any systematic patterning to the answers. Do not use three true items followed by three false items or any other systematic scheme. Incorporate some degree of randomness into the placement of true and false items. Above all, never use all true items or all false items.

11. Use a somewhat larger proportion of false items than true items. The reason for this admonition is that false items tend to be more discriminating than true items. This difference probably occurs because of the mental set with which a student approaches statements containing assertions. If the student does not possess the requisite knowledge to judge the truth or falsity of an assertion, and if the assertion is stated in forceful language, as most true-false items are, the student is more likely to answer true than false because of his conditioned respect for authoritative statements. If the statement is true and the student guesses "true," he will get the item correct when he should not. If the statement is false, however, and he guesses "true," he will miss the item as, in fact, he should.

12. Restrict true-false items to those important assertions or propo-

sitions which can be reasonably unambiguously judged true or false. The true-false form has been criticized on the basis of the "picky" nature of the knowledge it tests. This occurs because we do not know how to cast our major truths in true-false form. However, the true-false item can be a more versatile approach than it typically now is. We can test not only specific knowledge but also the ability to apply knowledge or principles to novel situations. Consider the following example:

T F   The magnitude of the standard deviation from a set of scores will be increased by five points if the magnitude of each of the scores is increased by five points.

The true-false form will undoubtedly continue to be one of the most popular of the item forms. The teacher should be aware, however, that it is really one of the most difficult forms to use well. Properly written, it can be a very effective type of item.

THE MULTIPLE-CHOICE FORM

Perhaps the most widely used item form is the *multiple-choice* form. It is certainly the form most frequently used by professional test writers, and its popularity among classroom teachers probably ranks it close to the essay form or the true-false form. Undoubtedly the major reason for its popularity is its versatility. This item form can be used to test almost any type of cognitive behavior from factual knowledge to the analysis of complex data. It is by all means the most flexible of the objectively scored item forms.

In format, the multiple-choice item consists of an introductory *stem*, which states the problem or asks the question, and a number of alternative answers or *responses* (usually 3–5) to this stem. One of these responses is the answer; the other alternatives are called *distractors* or *foils.*

In addition to its versatility, the multiple-choice item possesses other advantages when compared with objectively scored item forms. First of all, it yields more diagnostic information than true-false items. Through item analysis (which will be discussed in more detail in Chapter 7) we can discover which students selected which responses. This procedure can tell us some of the common mistakes made by students and perhaps help us identify the misconceptions they hold. Next, the multiple-choice form is more reliable. The chance of guessing the answer is only one out of four or five on a multiple-choice item, where it is one out of two on a true-false item. To the extent that chance is reduced as an operative factor, the reliability of a test is increased. Finally, multiple-choice items tend to be less ambiguous than true–false items. The supporting structure of stem plus responses helps the examinee see the point of the item even if it was rather poorly written. This latter statement should not be taken to mean that it is easier to write good multiple-choice items than good true-false items. Both are reasonably difficult jobs to do well.

TYPES OF MULTIPLE-CHOICE ITEMS

Part of the versatility of the multiple-choice item lies in the many variations this form can assume. Most of such variations are designed for special applications, however, so there would seem to be no compelling reason to discuss them in a book of this nature. But the teacher should be familiar with the basic varieties of this item form.

The correct-answer variety. This is the variety most people think of when they think of multiple-choice items. The distinguishing character-istic of this variety is that one of the responses must be unambiguously correct and the other responses unambiguously incorrect. Here is a simple example:

In what year did the Pilgrims found Plymouth Colony?

a. 1607

*b. 1620
 c. 1643
 d. 1667

In the foregoing item, we were testing simple factual knowledge. To demonstrate the versatility of the multiple-choice form, notice in the next example that the correct-answer variety can also be used to test application of a principle, in this case, the principle that addition of a constant to a set of measures does not change the variability of those measures.

What would be the effect on the standard deviation of a set of 100 test scores if five points were added to each score?

1. The standard deviation would increase by five points.
2. The standard deviation would increase by an amount equal to the square root of 0.05.
*3. There would be no effect; the standard deviation would remain the same.
4. There is no way of predicting the effect in advance of actual calculations.

The best-answer variety. In contrast to the correct-answer variety, where one response is always clearly correct, the "correctness" of the responses in the best-answer variety may vary by degrees. The job of the examinee is to arrange the responses in order of correctness and pick the best one. Here is an example:

Which of the following factors, if operative in a testing situation, would do *most* to lower the reliability of the test scores?

1. Fatigue on the part of the examinees
2. Excessive noise outside the testing room
*3. Inadequate number of items in the test
4. Insufficient time allotment for completion of the test

Note that each of the first three responses would adversely affect the reliability of the test results. In all likelihood, however, most damage would be done by a test which has too few items for the task intended.

The best-answer variety has been the butt of much criticism by individuals hostile to objective item forms. The major charge seems to be that good cases can be built for those responses which the item writer originally conceived to be second or even third best. This criticism may be valid where the item writer has made his responses too homogeneous in an attempt to achieve finer discriminations. Item writers should be aware of this possibility and should take care to see that what they key as the "answer" would also be chosen by the overwhelming majority of experts in the field.

The multiple-answer variety. It is, of course, possible to construct multiple-choice items on which more than one of the responses is correct and for which the student is instructed to mark all of the correct answers. Here is an example:

Which of the following Presidents of the United States also served as Vice-President? More than one answer may be correct.

1. Harry S Truman
2. Dwight D. Eisenhower
3. John F. Kennedy
4. Lyndon B. Johnson
5. Richard M. Nixon

It will be noted that such items are a variation of the correct-answer variety; more than one answer cannot be "best." Also, the scoring of such items is complicated by the fact that a penalty must be given for marking responses which are incorrect. Generally, the score is the number of answers marked correctly minus the number of responses marked incorrectly. If such a procedure is not employed, the student will soon learn to mark all responses.

Perhaps a better solution would be to recognize that the multiple-answer item is really an exercise consisting of a number of true-false items and to have the student mark each response on that basis.

The negative variety. The negative variety of multiple-choice item differs from the other varieties by asking that the examinee choose the response which does not answer the question correctly. The other responses give correct answers. The keyed answer does not. Here is a simple example:

Which of the following creatures is *not* a mammal?

1. The dog
*2. The dove
3. The mouse
4. The whale

The negative variety is seldom used by professional test writers. Yet, it is still very common in classroom tests. Why the difference?

The reason very likely is that the teacher finds it easy to construct this type of item when he is testing knowledge of a list of things he thinks the student ought to know. All he has to do is to select three or four items from the list and then supply another item worded in much the same fashion but not a part of the original list. The professional item writer, on the other hand, recognizes that this practice gives undue emphasis to negative learning. Teaching and learning should emphasize positive and important outcomes rather than negative ones.

In certain cases, however, negative learning may be important, and in such cases a negative approach could be justified. Consider the following item:

Which of the following practices is *not* recommended when a group of people are attempting to cross thin ice?

*1. Running rapidly
2. Carrying long sticks

3. Tying ropes to each other
4. Going one by one in single file

If the teacher does decide to use negatively worded items, he should be extremely careful to see that the "not" or other negative word employed is underlined or capitalized. If it is not, the student may fail to perceive that it is a negative question and choose the first correct response he discovers. This would cause him to miss the item.

APPROACHES TO WRITING THE MULTIPLE-CHOICE ITEM

The stem. The stem of a multiple-choice item is typically worded either as a direct question or as an incomplete sentence. In most cases, the same item idea can be written either way. Take this simple item:

When was Virginia Colony first settled?

a. 1592
b. 1600
c. 1607
d. 1620

The same item worded as an incomplete sentence looks like this:

Virginia Colony was first settled in

a. 1592.
b. 1600.
c. 1607.
d. 1620.

Which approach—question or incomplete sentence—should the item writer employ? Actually, there is no absolute answer to be given to this question. In most cases, it is probably better to write the stem as a question. This enables the item writer to spot any hidden ambiguities because then the statement has to stand by itself. Presumably, if the stem is written as a question, it should be capable of eliciting free responses from students. If there is some doubt concerning the meaning of the question or the type of answer which is appropriate, then the stem is not correctly written. There are certain cases, however, where the item is actually improved by writing the stem as an incomplete sentence. This will be particularly true where the writer can achieve an economy of words with no loss in clarity. If this can be done, then the incomplete sentence should certainly be used.

The responses.   There are normally three to five responses in a multiple-choice item.   All items do not need to have the same number of responses.   Standardized tests normally do, but this is because they typically use a "correction for guessing" formula for scoring the test. Since this is inadvisable for classroom tests, the number of responses per item can be allowed to vary.

Responses are designated either by numbers or letters, lowercase or capitals. If many of the items contain responses which are numbers, it is well to use letters to designate the responses. Incidentally, when this is the case, it is also advisable to word the item stem as a question to avoid terminal periods which may be mistaken for decimal points. If you are using a standard answer sheet of some sort, you will, of course, use the type of response designation required by the answer sheet.

Arrange the responses in a logical order if one exists or if there is no good reason to do otherwise. If, for example, the responses are numbers, arrange them in either ascending or descending order of magnitude. If the responses are the last names of individuals, place them in alphabetical order.

In most cases, it is advisable to arrange the responses vertically rather than horizontally. The horizontal arrangement is satisfactory if all of the items contain very short responses which do not take much space, such as this item:

What is the square root of 81?

(a) 6   (b) 7   (c) 8   (d) 9   (e) 10

Where the responses are longer, however, as they are in most items, the horizontal arrangement can pose reading difficulties for the student. Note what happens with a fairly typical item:

Why has Africa often been called the "Dark Continent"? (a) Many of the people of Africa are dark-skinned. (b) Very little was known of Africa for a long time. (c) The jungles of Africa are dark and forbidding. (d) Most of Africa is covered with "black earth" soils.

When writing such items it is much better to employ a vertical arrangement of the responses. Note how much easier the item is to read in this form.

Why has Africa often been called the "Dark Continent"?

a. Many of the people of Africa are dark-skinned.
b. Very little was known of Africa for a long time.
c. The jungles of Africa are dark and forbidding.
d. Most of Africa is covered with "black earth" soils.

The only major advantage of the horizontal arrangement is that it saves space. The saving of a few cents in paper, however, does not compensate for the loss in relevance which occurs by adding an extra burden of reading onto the student.

Punctuation. If you examine either standardized tests or teacher-made tests, you will find multiple-choice items punctuated in a myriad of ways. This only demonstrates that there is, as yet, no single, universally accepted method of punctuation. There is no good reason, however, why new methods of punctuation need be invented for test items. They are, after all, forms of English prose and should be punctuated as such. These three rules will cover most situations:

1. Where the stem is an incomplete sentence, there should be no terminal punctuation at the end of the stem. Each response, however,

should have appropriate terminal punctuation because it provides a possible ending to the incomplete sentence given in the stem.

2. Where the stem is a question, it should have a question mark as terminal punctuation. Each response should be punctuated according to its nature. If it is a complete sentence, it should be punctuated as one. If it is merely a date, a name, or a phrase, it should have no terminal punctuation.

3. The responses to items having incomplete sentences as stems should begin with lower-case letters. If the stem is a question, responses should begin with capital letters.

GENERAL SUGGESTIONS FOR WRITING MULTIPLE-CHOICE ITEMS

Inexperienced item writers frequently make a number of mistakes in writing multiple-choice items. The suggestions which follow will help you to avoid the most frequent of these mistakes.

1. Make sure that the stem of each item contains a clearly defined problem. Remember that the stem should be able to stand by itself and elicit free responses. If it cannot, in all likelihood the item is really a collection of true-false statements masquerading as a multiple-choice item. This is how such items usually look:

Admiral Byrd

1. was the hero of the Battle of Manila Bay.
2. was the first man to climb Mt. Everest.
3. was a famous Antarctic explorer.
4. explored the Virgin Islands and claimed them for England.

The item idea is a simple one—the identification of Admiral Byrd. It would be best to rewrite this item as a simple question.

Who was Admiral Byrd?

1. The commander of the American fleet at the Battle of Manila Bay

2. An Australian naval officer who became the first man to climb Mt. Everest

3. An American naval officer famed for his Antarctic explorations

4. A British naval officer who explored the Virgin Islands and claimed them for England

2. Do not use more words than necessary to make your meaning clear. To the extent that we allow our items to become too lengthy, we lower the relevance of our results by introducing reading speed and perhaps reading comprehension as irrelevant factors.

One way to economize on words is to avoid the inclusion of non-functional words in the item stem. These are usually additional words placed in the stem by the writer in order to provide background or "set the scene" for the item idea. In most cases, they are not necessary. They simply consume additional reading time. Here is an example:

Americans have typically shown a willingness to support public education. Some schools, however, receive more support than others. Where are the best financially supported schools located?

a. In the large cities
b. In the small towns
c. In the suburbs of large cities
d. In the rural areas

Most of the verbiage in this item is unnecessary. The item could be rewritten in this fashion with no loss in meaning:

Which type of public school typically receives the greatest financial support?

a. The big-city school
b. The small-town school
c. The suburban school
d. The rural school

Another method of economizing on words is to make sure that there is little or no wording in the responses which could not be more profitably included in the stem. Here is an example of uneconomical use of words:

How are members of school boards usually chosen?

a. They are elected by the voters.
b. They are elected by the City Council.
c. They are elected by other members of the board.
d. They are elected by the State Board of Education.

This item could be rewritten as follows:

Who elects the members of a local school board?

a. The voters
b. The City Council
c. The incumbent members of the board
d. The State Board of Education

3. Make sure that your responses are parallel in grammatical structure and that the structure you employ is one appropriate to the wording of the stem. Here is an item which violates both of these rules:

Why do we inoculate children with smallpox vaccine?

a. Some children have the disease
b. To keep them from getting the disease
c. For experimental purposes
d. Stop the spreading of germs

The grammatical form of the response should be one which comes naturally as a response to the stem. In the case of this item, the infinitive phrase would seem most appropriate. We could then rewrite the item as follows:

Why do we inoculate children with smallpox vaccine?

a. To cure children who already have the disease

b. To prevent children from getting the disease

c. To experiment on methods of curing the disease

d. To stop the spread of germs causing the disease

4. Do not allow your responses to overlap so that one response includes one or more other responses. Each response should present an independent option to the examinee. If it does not, the item is defective. Here is an example of such an item:

Where is the exact geographical center of the 48 contiguous states?

a. Near Topeka, Kansas

b. In the Midwest

c. In the Mississippi Valley

d. In the Missouri Valley

5. Try to keep all responses approximately the same length. At times this will be difficult if not impossible to do, but it should be observed as a general rule. Above all, never make the answer consistently longer, shorter, or of intermediate length in relation to the distractors. Students will discover any systematic pattern and use it as an irrelevant clue to the answer.

6. Avoid the use of either "None of these" or "All of these" as final responses. Teachers will frequently use one or the other (sometimes even both) of these two expressions as the fourth or fifth response for an item. Sometimes they do it because they cannot think of another plausible distractor. Sometimes they do it because they think it is a good thing to do. In either case, they should be disabused of the notion.

"None of these" has sometimes been recommended as an appropriate response for items calling for mathematical calculations. One argument advanced is that some able students may be able to answer an item correctly by approximating the answer and choosing the response nearest their approximation. If "None of these" is used as the correct answer very early in the test, they will soon learn not to do this. The counterargument is that approximation is a very useful skill which should not be discouraged. In any event, it would appear that if the ability to calculate is what is to be tested, the short-answer form is a more relevant approach than the multiple-choice form.

"All of these" has an even more tenuous claim to legitimacy. The teacher who uses this expression as a final response thinks that it promotes closer reading of the item and calls for more information in order to answer it correctly. The latter may be partially true; the former is doubtful. There are two major criticisms of the use of this expression. First, the student answering an item frequently reads no further than the point at which he discovers what he thinks is the correct answer. When "All of these" is used as a final response, the student may discover that the first response is correct and go no further. An even more telling criticism is that the use of "All of these" provides a clue to the sophisticated examinee. If he can recognize that any two of the initial responses are correct, he knows that "All of these" has to be the correct answer. Thus the other responses are strictly nonfunctional so far as he is concerned. Obviously, any irrelevant clue lowers the relevance of that particular item.

7. Vary the position of the answer, and have an approximately equal distribution of answers in the various response positions. Strict randomness of position for the answer is probably not necessary so long as no systematic pattern is used. Try not to have any lengthy "runs" on one response position for the answer. If the student marks position number three more than four times in a row, he may begin to doubt his own wisdom. It is not necessary to have exactly the same number of answers at every position, but any excessive deviation from this pattern may provide a clue to the perceptive examinee.

8. Do not allow the stem of the item to provide a clue to the correct response. This can occur in a number of ways. One of the simplest is the grammatical clue. Here is an example of an item where the stem calls for a plural response so that only one of the responses of this item is a reasonable answer.

What were the major factors underlying the rise of Nazism in Germany?

a. The political weakness of the Weimar Republic
b. The influence of fascism in Italy
c. Economic depression and strong feelings of nationalism
d. The military threat posed by Russia

Another error occurs when common elements in the stem and the correct answer provide an easy clue for the examinee. Here is an example:

What is an equation?

a. A mathematical expression where one side of the expression is equal to the other side of the expression
b. A type of circus performer who specializes in horseback riding
c. An athlete who performs as well with one hand as with the other hand
d. A legal document which specifies how the property of a person is to be divided among his heirs

THE MATCHING FORM

The *matching form* is a variant of the multiple-choice form. It consists of a number of items each of which has the same set of alternative responses. Such a set of items having a structural unity is called an *exercise*. In its usual format, a matching exercise consists of a set of *items* on the left side of the page and a set of *responses* on the right side of the page. The examinee is instructed to choose from the list of responses the one which is most closely associated with the item statement. Here is an example of a matching exercise:

DIRECTIONS: From the list of names at the right, choose the name of the person described in the statement at the left. Write the letter preceding this name in the blank space to the left of the item number. A name may be used as many times as necessary.

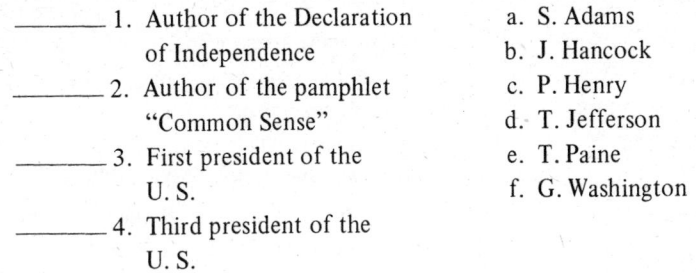

The major advantage of the matching exercise is its efficiency. If each of the statements in the preceding exercise had been used as the stem of a multiple-choice item, much more space would have been used on the test booklet, and much more of the examinee's time would have been required to read and respond to the items.

The major disadvantage of the matching exercise is the limited scope of knowledge it can be used to measure. It is best suited to the measurement of verbal associative knowledge. To the extent that a teacher's educational objectives specify this type of knowledge, the matching exercise can be an efficient tool for assessing its presence.

Simple as the matching exercise may appear to be, many errors can be committed in using it. The following section contains suggestions for avoiding such errors.

SUGGESTIONS FOR WRITING MATCHING ITEMS

1. Write very precise directions for the exercise. Do not simply say, "Match the items in column A with those in column B," or something similar. Describe the nature of both the items and the responses, and tell what the basis for the matching is to be. Then tell the examinee how he is to record his answers.

2. Always use the longer of the elements to be matched as the items and the shorter of the elements as the responses. Arranging the elements in this manner will reduce reading speed as an irrelevant factor in the exercise. Since the examinee must search among the responses for

the correct answer, it is advisable to have these responses as short as possible. If the longer elements are used as responses, it may double the time the examinee needs to spend on the exercise.

3. Use short lists of items and responses. There are several reasons for this suggestion. First, this practice also reduces the influence of reading speed as an irrelevant factor in the exercise. If the list of responses is long, say fifteen or more, the examinee must spend much of his time running his eye up and down the list. Second, it is difficult to maintain homogeneity of premises and responses with long lists. This problem will be discussed more thoroughly in suggestion number 4. Third, extremely long matching exercises may destroy the balance of a test and lower its relevance. The matching exercise is fairly easy to construct, and the item writer may be tempted to use more items than he should. This problem will also be more thoroughly discussed in suggestion number 8.

4. Use only homogeneous lists of items and responses. By this we mean that all items and responses should be drawn from the same general area. In other words, do not mix oranges and bananas. Here is an example of a faulty exercise:

_____ 1. Commander-in-chief of the American expeditionary force in World War I

_____ 2. Name of the famous battle of World War I

_____ 3. Date of Treaty of Versailles

_____ 4. Country where incident igniting World War I occurred

a. Marne
b. Pershing
c. Serbia
d. 1919

5. Use more responses than items. If the number of responses is the same as the number of items, then it is always possible that the examinee can get the last item in the exercise right by means of elimination. If this occurs, the relevance of the exercise is lowered. One way to ensure more responses than items, even with very short lists, is to tell

the examinee that responses may be used as frequently as necessary. This means they may be used once, more than once, or not at all.

6. Arrange the responses in logical order (e.g., alphabetical, chronological, magnitude) if such order exists. This will make it easier for the examinee to locate the response he is seeking and reduce reading time.

7. Keep the exercise intact on one page of the test booklet. Do not break it over two pages. The reason for this is again efficiency and reading speed. If the examinee must switch from one page to another, it increases the amount of time he must spend on the exercise and penalizes the student with slower perceptual speed.

8. Unless your test specifications call for heavy measurement of associative knowledge, do not make excessive use of matching exercises. It is all too easy to overdo items of this sort. You can probably think of certain facts your students ought to know. Then you can think of other related facts which might rather efficiently be combined into a matching exercise. Before you know it, you have spoiled the balance of your test and violated the strictures of your table of specifications. The matching exercise is a valuable approach to measurement when properly employed, but don't overdo it.

THE CLASSIFICATION FORM

The *classification form* of test item is similar to the matching form. In fact, many writers consider it a variety of the matching form. It is sufficiently different, however, that it deserves special treatment.

Like the matching form, the classification item is always found as part of an exercise. The exercise consists of a number of items which present names, observations, or other statements. Each such item is to be classified using a scheme which is usually presented immediately before the items. Here is a simple example:

Items 1–5 consist of names of famous men in American history. You are to choose the field of endeavor in which each man became famous using the scheme below. Place the letter of your answer in the blank provided to the left of the item number.

_____ 1. William Bryan   a. Inventor
_____ 2. Henry Clay   b. Military man
_____ 3. Thomas Edison   c. Politician
_____ 4. John McCormick
_____ 5. John Pershing

The advantage of the classification form over the usual matching form is its versatility. It can be used to measure simple verbal associations, as in the preceding exercise, or it can be used to measure complex cognitive skills. It is well-fitted to measuring some of the higher-level educational objectives such as application or interpretation. Consider, for example, the following exercise, which, according to Bloom,[1] measures the "ability to recognize what particulars are relevant to the validation of a judgment." Items 22–26 are to be judged in relation to this resolution:

Resolved: *That the term of the President of the U. S. should be extended to six years.*

Some statements in items 22 to 26 support the resolution, either directly or indirectly; some could be used in arguing against the resolution, and some have no bearing on the issue at all. Mark each statement

A. if you feel that it could be used by the affirmative side in a debate on the resolution.
N. if you feel that it could be used by the negative side.
X. if you feel it has no bearing on either side of the argument.

(Note: You are not asked to judge the truth or falsity of the resolution or the statements.)

_____ 22. Efficiency increases with experience.
_____ 23. According to the principles upon which the U. S. was founded, the people should have a frequent check on the President.

[1] Benjamin S. Bloom, *Taxonomy of Educational Objectives*, p. 160.

_____ 24. The party system has many disadvantages.

_____ 25. During most of a presidential election year, the economic life of a nation is depressed by the uncertainty as to the outcome.

_____ 26. The people should have the opportunity to keep a satisfactory President as long as they wish.

The classification form is not so widely used by teachers as it should be. Like the multiple-choice form it possesses versatility of application. Like the matching form, it is economical of space.

THE ESSAY FORM

Of all forms of written test items, the *essay form* is most senior. The written examinations of a century ago consisted exclusively of items of this type. It was not until the twentieth century that the "new" examinations appeared. With the introduction of the newer "objective" item forms, a certain disenchantment developed for the older essay form. The weaknesses of the essay form as a measurement device were revealed in study after study. As a consequence, it is difficult today to find a professionally prepared test which uses essay items.

Though it may not be popular with the professionals, the essay item continues to be widely used by teachers. Why? In the first place, it takes much less time to write essay items than to write objective items. Time is a commodity in short supply for most teachers. It takes only a minute or two to jot down on a stencil a few items which seem reasonable and to reproduce enough copies for the entire class. If the teacher is really pressed, the items can simply be written on the chalkboard. In the second place, the writing of essay items appears to demand no special training or skill. The typical teacher feels that he knows his material sufficiently well to phrase several questions eliciting the type of response he is seeking. In the third place, the essay item form has not been closely associated with such technical notions as validity, reliability, difficulty, or discrimination. Essay items were here long before these notions arose, and it seems almost sacrilegious to insist that they be applied to this item form. The teacher feels he need not concern himself with such esoteric ideas when using essay items. Lastly, the essay item requires writing and recall. We have already discussed the position taken by many teachers that recall is superior to recognition as a form of memory. In addition, exclusive of the short-answer item, the essay item is the only item form requiring writing. Since skill in writing is deemed a valuable type of achievement, the essay item has an inherent advantage.

With such apparent advantages, why is the essay item shunned by the professionals? In the first place, they have discovered that it is not so easy to write as it first appears. Like true-false items, essay items can be written quickly but sloppily. A teacher examining the items written by another teacher may find them to be vague, ambiguous, unstructured, or even misleading. Most teachers have had this experience. To be good, essay items need to be written carefully with much thought given to the precise type of task to be presented in the item. But by far the major drawbacks of the essay item, from the point of view of the professional, are the weaknesses associated with scoring. The first such weakness is the relatively large amount of time needed to score such items satisfactorily. The second, and more important weakness, is the unreliability of the scoring.

Reliability. The reliability of scoring of an essay item is usually demonstrated in one of two ways: (1) interscorer reliability, or (2) intrascorer reliability. The first requires that two or more readers score the item independently. The correlation between the independent scorings gives an estimate of the reliability of the scoring procedures. In the second approach, the same reader scores the item twice, usually after a sufficient lapse of time so no contamination might result from memories of the first scoring. A correlation coefficient is then computed using the first and second scorings as the basic data. Typically, the reliability of scoring of essay items using these procedures is rather low, in the neighborhood of 0.50 or less.

The reliability of scoring for an essay test should not be confused with the reliability of the test itself. This can be easily understood if we contrast the essay examination with the objective examination. The reliability of scoring for an examination composed exclusively of objective items would be very high whether we used interscorer reliability or intrascorer reliability. The only reason we should expect less than perfect reliability would be because of clerical errors. If the scoring were done by machine, even these might be eliminated. But no one would argue that this perfect correlation coefficient thus obtained was the best possible index of the reliability of the test. They would insist that the regular procedures (test-retest, equivalent forms, split-halves) be employed to estimate such reliability. Unfortunately, these procedures are not so readily employed with essay tests. In the rare cases where they are employed it can be shown that the reliability of the test is not the same as the reliability of the scoring. Test reliability tends to be lower than reader reliability.[2]

Relevance. Despite the acknowledged low reliability of essay tests, it is evident that they provide the most relevant means of assessing certain educational outcomes. This is particularly true at the highest level of cognitive objectives, synthesis and evaluation. At these levels we are normally much more interested in whether the student can "produce" certain types of outcomes (e.g., a critical review of a novel) rather than whether he can distinguish between appropriate and inappropriate evaluations (though we may be interested in this also). To the extent that the essay item demands written production, it is relevant to the objective.

It should be made clearly apparent that the essay item is *not* the most relevant approach to testing knowledge. The possession of knowledge is tested both more relevantly and reliably through other item forms. The essay item is inefficient for the purpose. Yet if you were to examine

[2] William C. Budd, "An Experimental Comparison of Writing Achievement in English Composition and Humanities Classes," in *Research with Teaching of English*, Vol. 3, No. 2 (Fall 1969), pp. 209–221.

most essay items written by teachers, you would find that this was what they were measuring.

It might be well to consider at this point an argument which is often offered in support of essay items. Certain critics of modern education claim that the increasing use of objective items with the resultant displacement of the essay item has resulted in a lowered level of writing ability in modern students. Two points might be made in this connection. First, the evidence to support the assertion is tenuous at best. Since a larger proportion of children are now enrolled in school than was true 50 years ago, we would expect a lower level of achievement for the median student. Given students of equal education, however (high-school seniors in the college preparatory curriculum), there is little evidence that they write more poorly than their counterparts of a half-century ago. Second, it may be something of an exaggeration to credit the essay item with the ability to develop good writing in students. Everyone is aware that the best conditions for writing are not present in the examination room. It is unlikely that even the critics who extol the virtues of the essay item for this purpose do so by writing furiously at 8:01 A.M. on a topic handed to them the moment before. The ability to write well is important, but it is probably better developed under other arrangements. The most that can be said for the essay item is that it does reinforce the idea that writing is important and provides an opportunity for the student to practice skills which should have been acquired in a more leisurely fashion elsewhere.

SUGGESTIONS FOR THE USE OF ESSAY ITEMS

1. Restrict the use of essay items to those educational outcomes for which they provide the most relevant measures. Remember that if it is knowledge you wish to test, it can be tested equally relevantly and much more reliably with objective-item forms.

2. Be explicit in the task you present to the students. Do not use large, unrestricted questions such as: "Discuss the economic results of

World War II." Set a more precise task. Ask, for example: "What are the three most significant changes which have occurred in the world economy as a result of World War II, and what are the current effects of those changes?" Even this question is somewhat broader than it might be, but it does have the effect of focusing the attention of the student on a specific task.

3. Give your students practice in writing answers to essay items. This is not a skill which students learn automatically. Neither is there evidence of a direct transfer from the type of expository writing taught in English classes to the writing of answers to test items. It is a skill which should be taught and practiced. Give your students a sample item or two; demonstrate how they should answer such an item; give them another on which to practice; and if you have time, grade it for them. You should see improvement.

4. Provide sufficient time for students to compose and write a reasonable answer to the item. Most teachers underestimate the amount of time needed to write the answers. Remember that the student needs some time to think about the item before he starts to write. Try writing an answer yourself; time your effort, and add 50 percent to your time. This should give a reasonable approximation of the amount of time to give to the student. Remember that if you do not allow sufficient time, writing speed may become an irrelevant factor in this test.

5. Do not use optional items. This is a very common practice. A teacher will present five items and require the student to write on any two of the five. Teachers apparently do this to provide better "coverage" of the material—in other words, a broader sample. Generally this occurs, however, when the teacher is doing what he should not be doing, that is, using essay items to measure knowledge rather than higher-level cognitive skills. If you restrict your essay items to the latter type of cognitive behavior, the problem of providing a broad sample does not become so acute. Rather than increasing the validity of the sample, as many teachers believe, optional items actually decrease it. In order to obtain valid comparisons among students, each has to be

addressing himself to the same task. If 25 students are writing on 25 different combinations of items (which is entirely possible) how can you make valid comparisons?

6. Some teachers follow a practice of presenting a list of potential essay items to a class some time prior to the examination. They tell the students that the examination will consist of two or three items drawn from this list. This procedure has a number of things to recommend it. First, it enables the student to think about the items and formulate possible answers ahead of time. This is a more relevant type of writing from the point of view of long-range objectives. Typically, when we write anything, we have an opportunity to think about the topic ahead of time and formulate, even if only mentally, what it is that we plan to say. Second, unlike an out-of-class paper which might be written by someone else, the essay test has to be written under your supervision. It is somewhat similar to a class paper in English except that you are judging it on different criteria. You can see how well the student can prepare to write on certain topics when he knows what these are, how well he can organize his presentations, and how skillfully he can make his presentation. Since all students are assigned the same task, you can also make valid comparisons among students.

SUGGESTIONS FOR SCORING ESSAY ITEMS

As we have already pointed out, the most serious deficiencies of the essay item lie in the low reliability of the scoring process used for these items. Anything which can be done, then, to improve the reliability of the scoring process will result in improved testing practice.

There are two general approaches to the scoring of essay items, the *analytic* approach and the *sorting* approach. We will give suggestions for improving practice under both approaches.

The analytic approach. Basically, the analytic approach is an attempt to break the answer to an essay item down into *scoring units*. Such units are specified before the papers are read, and each paper is read to determine the quantity (and perhaps quality) of such units present in the paper. The units may have differential weighting, that is, some may carry more points of credit than others because the teacher deems them to be more important. When using this procedure, the teacher usually begins by preparing a *model* answer to the item. He then breaks this model down into the scoring units, that is, the facts, ideas, generalizations, principles, etc., that he will look for in scoring student responses. He assigns what he feels are the appropriate weights for each scoring unit and formulates some basis for distinguishing qualitatively as well as quantitatively within scoring units. Then he proceeds to score the papers, assigning scores by units for each item and summing item scores to obtain a total score for the examination.

The analytic approach is better suited to the so-called restricted-response type. The difference between these two types is largely a matter of degree. In the restricted-response type we specify in greater detail the manner in which the student is to respond and the details to which he is to address himself. In the extended-response type, we allow him more latitude in his manner of answering. Perhaps these two examples will illustrate the difference.

Restricted response

Make a brief comparison of the characterization of Agamemnon by Homer in *The Iliad* and by Aeschylus in *Agamemnon.* Write one short paragraph on each of the following points:

a. Major details of personality or character depicted
b. Major accomplishments reported
c. Opinion held of him by others
d. Sympathy of treatment by the author

Extended response

Read the following review of Camus' *The Stranger* written some 20 years ago by an eminent American critic. On which points do you agree with this critic, and on which points do you disagree with him?

When using the analytic approach, certain precautions should be taken. First, after constructing your model answer and your scoring units, read a few student papers selected at random and see how the key fits. Sometimes you will find that one or both of two things has occurred. The students may have interpreted the item differently than you intended, and so their answers tend to take a different turn. This is largely your fault as an item writer, but there is nothing you can do about that at this specific moment except to make allowances for it in your key. Another thing is that certain students, most likely the better ones, have stated additional points which could just as well be given credit. You may have to add these to your key. Second, once your key is finally formulated, stick to those points for your scoring. Do not allow extraneous factors such as penmanship, spelling, grammatical errors, or general writing ability influence your scoring. To the extent that these factors are allowed to influence the final score, the relevance of the score is affected. If you feel that these factors are important, then score the paper twice, once on content factors and once on other factors. Weight each score appropriately and combine them for a total score.

The sorting approach. As the name indicates, the basic procedure in the sorting approach is to sort student papers into piles on the basis of the quality of the response. Papers are read in a "holistic" fashion to discern the general quality of the paper. No attempt is made to isolate the individual elements contributing to this general quality. Obviously, this approach is more appropriate to extended-response items than to restricted-response items.

Teachers differ in the number of piles they use for the initial sorting. Most use three; some use five. A second reading is a necessity. The second reading serves two purposes. First, it helps to confirm or correct the initial sorting. Mistakes in judgment can be made, especially in judging the first few papers one reads. Second, it helps the teacher make further and finer differentiations among papers. The original three piles can be extended to nine piles by taking each and differentiating three degrees of quality within it. This is probably about the limit of refinement we can expect.

Some teachers prefer to use the second reading differently. They will record the result of their first sorting, lay the papers aside for a short while (not too long so their instructional value is impaired), and then sort them again (after shuffling) to get a second score. They will then average (or sum) the two scores for a final score. The principle involved here is that the average of two measures is more reliable than either of the two measures taken by itself.

There are certain precautions teachers should employ when using the sorting approach to scoring essay items.

1. If an examination consists of more than one essay item (and most will), sort the papers separately on each item. In other words, read and sort all papers on the first item; record your scoring; shuffle the papers; read and sort on the second item. Follow this procedure for each item. The major reason for this procedure is to randomize certain errors associated with the reading process. Among such errors are (1) the tendency of the standard of quality expected by the teachers to shift somewhat during the reading process, (2) the presence of fatigue in the scorer, and (3) the operation of halo effect. Halo effect occurs in this context when the quality of the response to one item biases the scorer's judgment on other items. If all items are read at the same reading, a student who does a particularly good job on the first item may have an unwarranted advantage over the student who muffs the initial item. Reading all papers for one item at a time will remove this possible source of bias.

2. If possible, read and sort the papers without knowledge of who wrote the paper. This can be done by having students write their names only on the back of the paper so when the paper is folded open, you

cannot see the name without turning the paper over. To do this successfully, you must learn to inhibit your natural curiosity. Of course, once you learn the handwriting of your students, even this procedure will not work. The reason for anonymous reading is, again, to reduce the operation of the halo effect. In this case, the halo effect operates through the teacher's general impression of a student. If the teacher judges a student to be superior or even just better than average, he is likely to receive a higher rating for an inferior response than will a student judged to be inferior, even though the responses may be almost identical in content.

3. Try to avoid allowing irrelevant factors to influence your rating of an item. Handwriting is the most pernicious of such factors. Spelling, grammar, and syntax also exert their influence. This is a very difficult thing to do. Studies have demonstrated that even when teachers are told to ignore such factors, they have difficulty in doing so.[3] This should not stop them from trying.

[3] D. P. Scannell and J. C. Marshall, "The Effect of Selected Composition Errors on Grades Assigned to Essay Examinations," *Am. Ed. Res. J.*, 3, 125 (1966).

6
ASSEMBLING AND SCORING OBJECTIVE EXAMINATIONS

The task of producing an examination does not end with the writing of the items. Items, once written, must be assembled into an examination. Although this might appear a relatively simple and straightforward task, there are many errors which the inexperienced test constructor can commit. The purpose of this chapter is to help avoid such errors.

ASSEMBLING THE EXAMINATION

Let us begin by assuming that a teacher has written a number of test items in accordance with a table of specifications. These items were probably written over a period of time prior to the date set for assembling the examination. The immediate task is to produce a copy of that examination. A better copy will be produced if the teacher follows the suggestions given in this chapter.

Editing of items. Before you finally decide to include an item in an examination, it should be given a final, thorough editing. Frequently, you will find that an item which appeared perfectly acceptable when originally written and even after being rewritten, now has defects which you have overlooked. As you read each item again, ask yourself these questions:

1. Is the wording of the item perfectly clear? Are any of the words ambiguous or misleading? Is the item worded as succinctly as possible with no loss in meaning? Does the item employ the simplest possible sentence structure appropriate to the meaning of the item idea? Is the vocabulary level of the item consonant with the vocabulary level of the students?

2. Does the item really do the job called for by the table of specifications? Is there any doubt as to the task set before the student in this item? Is it really measuring application or analysis as you intended and not some simple factual knowledge? Is this the most relevant way to measure this outcome, or should this item idea be cast in a different item form?

3. Do any of the items overlap? Are two of the items measuring exactly the same thing in essentially the same way? Does one item provide an answer to another item?

Reject or rewrite any items which do not pass this final editing. You must be careful to ensure that the items which survive fit your table of specifications reasonably well. They may not fit exactly, but slight adjustments in the number of items assigned to each cell in the table will not produce an undue distortion from your original intent.

Providing for identification. Once the items to be used have been chosen, the next task is to provide certain elements of identification for the test. The usual ones are these:

1. The name of the test, e.g., "Test on Romantic Poetry."
2. A place for the student to write his name, if you wish to have him do so. Also, provide a space for the date, if you desire it.
3. The form of the test, if it is one of two or more equivalent forms.

Ordering the items. Next you must decide on the order in which the items should appear. These suggestions will help you make decisions on item order.

1. Group all items of each item form together. Do not mix true-false items with multiple-choice items or any other type of item form. Each item form demands its own type of mental set, and the student should not be forced continually to switch mental sets as he proceeds from item to item.
2. Within each item form, group the items in some logical fashion. Some authors recommend ordering items by degree of difficulty, but there are two objections to this. First, if the item is a new one, it is difficult to judge accurately its difficulty level. Second, ordering items by difficulty level may result in a sequence which appears illogical to the student. The items jump from one topic to another in no apparent, systematic fashion. Besides, one of the aims of the item writer is to produce only items of moderate levels of difficulty, so there should be no great variability in item difficulty. The best approach is probably a topical arrangement. For each topic, concept, or principle tested, you may wish to order the items in accordance with Bloom's *Taxonomy*. That is, you may wish to place items calling for knowledge first, followed by items testing comprehension, application, and analysis later. Of course, if there is only one item on a given topic, or if all items are at the same cognitive level, the task of ordering items is somewhat simplified.
3. Decide upon the sequence of item forms. A given test normally should not include more than two or three different types of item

forms. There is some reason to believe that the simpler types of item forms should come first in a test. For example, if a test is to consist of matching, multiple-choice, and true-false items, the preferred arrangement might be true-false, matching, multiple-choice.

Writing directions. One of the most crucial parts of a test is the directions given to the students. Yet, it is one of the parts treated most lightly by teachers. Frequently they will not even include any directions, simply assuming that the students know what to do. This can be a mistake. Every student should have full opportunity to apply his knowledge and skills to the tasks contained in the items. If, because of inadequate directions, he is confused as to what it is that he is to do, the resulting test score will not be a relevant measure of his achievement.

There are two types of directions in a test. The first type consists of general directions given at the beginning of the test which apply to the entire test. The second type consists of specific directions given at the beginning of each part of the test.

In writing general directions, the teacher should attempt to anticipate questions which students might raise. Some of these might be:

1. Is there only one correct answer?

2. Where do I record my answers, on the test booklet or on an answer sheet?

3. How much time do I have for the test and for each part of the test?

4. Will my answers be corrected for guessing?

5. May I write on the test booklet?

6. If I have to make calculations, shall I make them on the test booklet or on a separate piece of scratch paper?

7. What do I do if I finish the test ahead of time?

The teacher decides which of these questions should be answered and provides the answers as part of the general directions.

The most important thing to remember when writing directions for the several parts of the test is to be specific. Tell the student exactly what it is that he is to do. This includes directions on how to read the items and how to record his answers. Do not use general and vague wording such as, "Associate the expressions in column B with those in column A," for a matching exercise. Describe what A and B are, tell the student the basis for the association, and tell him where to put his answer after he has made his selection. Specific examples of instructions for each type of item form were given in the previous chapter.

In testing younger children, the teacher may need to take even additional precautions to ensure that each student knows what it is that he is to do. An example of each item form as part of the directions for each new part of the test may be a big help. With very young children (first or second graders), the teacher may need to give the directions orally while the student reads the written directions on his test booklet.

Spacing. Many teachers do not give adequate attention to the spacing of items and directions on the test booklet. The result is a booklet which is not only esthetically unappealing but may be a handicap to the student. Anything which handicaps the student unnecessarily is an irrelevant factor in the test. The teacher should follow these suggestions on spacing:

1. Do not crowd your items too closely together. Always have at least one full typewriter space between items. Two spaces would be better.

2. Leave sufficient space for margins at the side of the paper. You may wish to use this space for recording answers. In any event, the test looks better with adequate margins.

3. Use extra space between parts of the test. Use a heading such as, "Part II—Multiple-Choice," followed by appropriate directions. Sometimes a line may be drawn part way across the page to separate one part from another.

4. Never break items in two, placing one part of the stem at the

bottom of a page and the remainder at the top of the following page. This only gives a slipshod appearance to the test, and it forces the student to spend extra time flipping from one page to the next.

5. Never break a matching exercise over two pages. Arrange your items in such a way that all elements of the exercise are on the same page.

6. Try to avoid breaking a classification exercise over two pages. This is not so catastrophic as breaking a matching exercise, but it is best not to do it if a little better planning can avoid it. If a break cannot be avoided, the responses should be repeated on the new page.

Provisions for recording answers. One of the advantages of using objective-item forms is the presumed facilitation of scoring. This facilitation will not occur, however, unless the teacher makes deliberate provisions for it. This can be done in several ways.

One of the easiest ways to facilitate scoring is to use a separate answer sheet. Such answer sheets can be used beginning at grades three or four. Prior to that time, it is probably better to have students record their answers directly on the test booklet. If separate answer sheets are used, they can be of the commercially prepared variety or of the homemade variety. The latter will be considerably less expensive and probably just as useful with the typical class of 30–35 students. The teacher can prepare a stencil for a format which will be useful for most item forms. A format such as the following would provide answer sheets applicable to multiple-choice, true-false, classification, and even short matching exercises.

Item no.	Response
1	A B C D E
2	A B C D E
3	A B C D E
4	A B C D E
5	A B C D E
Etc.	

In using a homemade answer sheet of this type, it is better to have the student cross out (X) his chosen response rather than encircle it. A circle may not always be detected when scoring with the punched key normally used with such answer sheets.

If you do not wish to use a separate answer sheet, you will probably wish the students to record their answers directly in the test booklet. When you do this, you can facilitate scoring by following these suggestions:

1. Provide blanks in either the right- or left-hand margin of the test booklet. Instruct students to place their answers in these blanks. From the viewpoint of the student, blanks in the right-hand margin are preferable. This preference follows logically from left-to-right sequence of reading and because, for most students (the majority are right-handed), the process of writing in the right margin will not obscure the reading of test items to the left. If blanks are to be used in the right-hand column, it may be necessary to provide leaders (. . . . .) from the end of the item to the blank. The blank is sometimes also enclosed in parentheses to set it off from the body of the test. When using the completion variety of short-answer item, it may be useful to use a series of dashes (- - - - -) in the context of the sentence where the word has been deleted so the student will not be tempted to write his answer in that space.

It is probably easier for the teacher to place the blanks to the left of the item number, particularly if he is cutting his own stencil. As far as ease of scoring is concerned, it does not seem to make too much difference whether blanks are in the right or left margin.

2. Use a *strip key* for scoring when answers are recorded directly in the test booklet. The easiest way to make such a key is simply to take an unused copy of the test, record the correct answers in red pencil (or any other color different from the usual blue or black used by students), and lay the key directly alongside the student's responses. Then you can mark either the correct or the incorrect answers as you prefer. By force of training, it seems more logical to us to mark the incorrect answers. Marking correct answers, however, will enable you to get a

score for that page simply by counting your marks. No subtraction of wrong answers from number of items on the page will be needed. Score one page at a time, flipping the page over after you have scored it. After you have scored the last page, sum the results for all pages and obtain a total score.

Proofreading. Whether you cut your own stencils or not, you should proofread them carefully. Minor typographical errors can be a source of confusion. Read each word to see that it is spelled properly. Check the numbering of the items. Sometimes when you go from the bottom of one page to the top of the next, you will repeat the same number for two consecutive items. If you are using separate answer sheets, the resulting confusion can be traumatic. Careful proofreading can pay large dividends.

SCORING

Normally, test items are scored as either right or wrong, and the score for the test is the number of items answered correctly. Sometimes, however, teachers wonder whether test scores should be *corrected for guessing*. The formula used for this process is given as:

$$S = R - \frac{W}{N-1},$$ (6.1)

where S is the score after correction for guessing, R is the number of items answered correctly, W is the number of items answered incorrectly, N is the number of alternative responses in the item form.

Using a 100-item true-false test as an example, a student who answered 70 items correctly, missed 20, and omitted 10, would obtain a corrected score of 50, calculated as follows:

$$S = 70 - \frac{20}{2-1} = \frac{50}{1} = 50.$$

The best advice to teachers considering the use of the correction-for-guessing formula is to forget it. There are valid reasons for this advice. First, a basic assumption underlying the use of the formula is that all guessing on test items is random guessing. This is far from the case. When students guess, they usually guess on the basis of partial knowledge which is not sufficient to allow them to choose the correct answer unequivocally. They will hesitate and then make a reasoned guess. Reasoned guesses will always beat the formula. Second, if all students answer all items, which will likely be the case with most classroom achievement tests, there will be a perfect correlation between corrected and uncorrected test scores. Since the relative position of the student in the class is of more importance to us than the specific raw score he obtained on the test, correcting for guessing has gained us nothing but additional labor. Third, there is no good educational reason to penalize guessing, particularly reasoned guessing. It is something we must all do all our lives, and the more proficient we become at it, the better off we will be. Correction-for-guessing formulas are most appropriately used with speeded tests. Since classroom achievement tests should be power tests rather than speeded tests, it is better to use uncorrected scores.

Teachers also wonder whether they should assign differential scoring weights to items. Some items may be testing something which seems more important than that which is tested by other items. Should we not give two points for a correct answer to such items? Again, the answer is no. It is not worth the extra effort. Studies of weighted scoring have rather conclusively demonstrated that the use of differential item weights adds nothing to the validity of test scores. If you wish to weight certain aspects of achievement more heavily than others, use additional items to measure those aspects. But score each item only as either right or wrong. It will make life much simpler.

7
ITEM
ANALYSIS

Up to this point, we have been talking about the kinds of things a teacher should do prior to the time a test is administered. In this and the next chapter, we shall be talking about what should be done after a test is administered.

We have commented from time to time about the difficulty of constructing good objective tests. Many teachers make the job even more difficult by starting from scratch each time they build a test. There is really no good reason to do this. Test items, once written, can be used again and again. They should only be used, however, if it can be demonstrated that they are *good* test items. The procedures of item analysis, which we propose to discuss in this chapter, provide the means to discover the worth of individual test items.

Item analysis is a set of procedures by which we demonstrate how effectively a given test item functions within the total test. Each item is an element within a test, a part of a larger whole. In a sense, it is a test within a test, and the validity of the entire test is dependent upon the validity of each of these smaller tests. One of the major functions of item analysis is to provide us with an estimate of the validity of each item.

The major purpose of item analysis is to discover which items are functioning well and which are functioning poorly. Once we identify the latter, we can then study these defective items in an attempt to isolate the reasons for their malaise, and, if we think them remediable, revise them for subsequent use. If we do a good job of revision, the items may function much better the next time. Perhaps we may discover that the reason an item is not functioning well does not reside within the item. It may be a deficiency within the class or—heaven forbid—within our instruction. If either hypothesis is tenable, we should take steps to remedy the source of the deficiency, whatever it might be.

Item analysis also helps teachers to become better item writers. Item writing is a skill which can be improved through practice. As in learning any other skill, however, some feedback is necessary. We need to know how well we are doing. The results from item analyses will give us some of the feedback we need. Such results can tell us, for example, whether we have pitched the difficulty level of the item correctly, whether we have written plausible distractors, and even, perhaps, whether we have overlooked some source of ambiguity in an item. These are things we ought to know.

Item analysis provides us with three basic types of information:

1. information about the difficulty of the time;
2. information about the discriminating power of the item; and
3. information about the pattern of responses to the item.

We shall discuss each of these types of information in remaining sections of this chapter.

PREPARING FOR AN ITEM ANALYSIS

It is easier to make item analyses if separate answer sheets are used for the test. If that is the case, you begin an item analysis by arranging the answer sheets in rank order of score from high to low. Having completed this ranking, you select about one-fourth to one-third of the answer sheets from the top of the class and an equal number from the bottom of the class.[1] The answer sheets from the middle of the class will not be used. The exact number of answer sheets you select is of no great importance. If the class contains about 30 students, you may wish to have ten papers in each of your groups in order to facilitate the simple calculations which will be involved. Having selected these papers, you then proceed to record the manner in which the students whose papers you have selected responded to each of the test items. The data thus recorded provide the basis for the item analysis.

In our own work, we have found it advantageous to record our data in a form which is given in Fig. 7.1. This form is constructed primarily for use with multiple-choice items, but it can be used for true-false, classification, or even matching items. It provides space to record the

Figure 7.1 Item analysis form.

Date

Diff.		
Disc.		
Response	U	L
1		
2		
3		
4		
5		
Omit		

[1] Technically, the optimum proportion of the class for these two groups is 27%. Since it is usually difficult to obtain this exact percentage with a small class, and since slight deviations above or below it will not have too much effect on our relatively unrefined measures, we simply recommend any percentage in the near vicinity.

index of difficulty, the index of discrimination (both of which we will show you how to calculate), and the distribution of student responses to the several response positions of the item. The symbols "U" and "L" stand for "upper" and "lower," respectively; in other words, our high-ranking group and our low-ranking group selected from the top and bottom of our ranked scores.

Now it is appropriate that we proceed to a more detailed discussion of difficulty and discrimination and how knowledge of these factors can be used to improve the quality of test items.

DIFFICULTY

It is usual to express the difficulty of a test item by means of an *index of difficulty*. This index is given simply as the percentage of individuals attempting the item who answer it correctly. In a sense, this method of calculating the index is unfortunate because the resulting value gives the "ease" of the item rather than its difficulty. That is, an item with an index of 40 percent is more difficult than an item with an index of 60 percent. However, the practice of calculating the index in this fashion is now so firmly entrenched that it would be difficult to change it.

When we calculate the index of difficulty for an item using our item-analysis data, we use only the information from the two groups, the high and the low, that we have selected from our class. We do not use the information from the students in the middle.[2] To obtain our index of difficulty, we combine the data from the two extreme groups. If, for example, we had ten persons each in our high and low groups, we would determine the number of correct answers in each group, add them, and divide by 20. We would multiply the resulting decimal fraction by 100 to convert it to a percentage and call the product our index of difficulty. Suppose, in this example, eight of the upper group

[2] The reasoning behind this procedure is that the numerical value produced by averaging the two extreme groups will be approximately that which we would obtain if we used the data from the entire class. Empirical investigations have demonstrated that this assumption holds true.

and six of the lower group answered correctly. We would sum eight and six, divide by 20, and multiply by 100. The result would be 70 percent, which would be the numerical value of our index.

One factor which we have to take into account in calculating indexes of difficulty is the matter of *omits*. What do we do when a student does not answer an item? What we do depends on where the omitted item occurs. If it occurs in the main part of the test and the student has answered items subsequent to the omitted item, we count an omit as a wrong answer. We assume that he had a chance to read and attempt the item but chose not to do so. If the omit occurs at the end of the test, however, such an assumption seems unwarranted. The student probably ran out of time. Hence, we do not count such omits as wrong answers but assume that the student did not attempt the item.

Of what value is an index of difficulty? There are several answers to this question. The first is that knowledge of the difficulty levels of test items allows us to control the shape of the distribution of scores we will get from a test composed of such items. The logic behind this is fairly self-evident if you consider the following situation. Suppose you were asked by your school principal to construct a test which would help select a group of potential honors students for a new class. To do this, you would want the distribution of scores to be positively skewed, that is, to look like Fig. 7.2. You would want such a distribution in order to have maximum reliability at the high end of the scale of achievement. The scores of most students would pile up toward the low end of your

Figure 7.2 Positively skewed distribution produced by a test composed exclusively of difficult items.

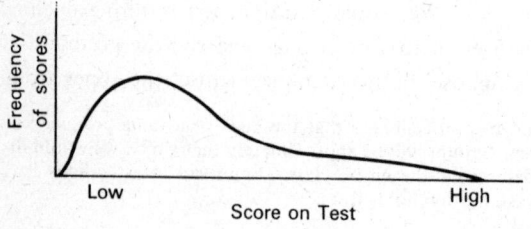

scale, but since these persons would not be considered honors candidates, it would make little difference to you if they were all lumped closely together. It is only at the top of the scale that you need precision. How could you produce a positively skewed distribution of test scores? The answer is simple—by using nothing but very difficult test items. The scores of the few students who could respond reasonably successfully to a series of very difficult items would form the "tail" of your positively skewed distribution. Conversely, we would produce a negatively skewed distribution by using nothing but easy items. This will be the case in the typical *mastery* or *diagnostic* test, where we wish to discover how well our students have mastered the material we expected them to learn.

At this point it might be well to distinguish between a mastery test and a test of *relative achievement* which is the type of test we are most concerned with in this book. A mastery test is essentially an instructional tool. When we use such a test, we are concerned with the extent to which our students have mastered certain materials which we feel are basic to further work in this area. Typically the items in such tests are knowledge items rather than items calling for higher types of cognitive skills. They also tend to be reasonably easy items. We assume that if fewer than 90 percent of the class answer an item correctly, there may have been some deficiency in learning or perhaps in teaching. Thus, the results of such a test supply us with diagnostic information.

But an achievement test serves a different purpose. The function of an achievement test is to spread student scores along the continuum of achievement as widely and as reliably as possible. Only if we do this can we assume that we are capable of making reliable distinctions among students with reference to their relative achievement. In other words, we wish to produce maximum variability in order to increase the accuracy of our measurements.

How can we achieve this maximum spread of scores we are seeking? By using items of moderate difficulty. The best level of difficulty for an item is 50 percent. Items of this level make the maximum number of discriminations among students and produce the greatest variability in test scores.

Though a difficulty index of 50 percent is considered best, we must add certain qualifications. The first is that this figure refers to a *corrected* index of difficulty. What does this mean? Suppose we consider the case of true-false items. Theoretically, students have a 50 percent chance of guessing the answer to a true-false item in the absence of any relevant knowledge. Consequently, the minimum index of difficulty we might expect for such an item would be the *chance* or 50 percent level. The maximum would obviously be 100 percent. We could correct the obtained difficulty level of a true-false item by using the correction-for-guessing formula discussed in the previous chapter. In this case the formula would appear as follows:

$$\text{Corrected difficulty} = \%R - \frac{\%W}{N-1}, \tag{7.1}$$

where $\%R$ is the percentage answering correctly, $\%W$ is the percentage answering incorrectly, and N is the number of alternative responses on the item.

Using the formula we could demonstrate that an uncorrected index of 75 percent for a true-false item is equal to a corrected index of 50 percent.

$$75\% - \frac{25\%}{2-1} = 50\%.$$

In the type of simplified item analysis which we are proposing in this book, there is no great need to correct our indices of difficulty. We can estimate the *median* difficulty level for our items by taking a point halfway between the chance level for that type of item and perfect performance. If, for example, our test consisted of four-response multiple-choice items, the chance level would be 25 percent, and a point halfway between 25 percent and 100 percent would be approximately 63 percent. The figure of 63 percent, then, would establish median difficulty for such items.

A second thing we must remember is that it is impossible to have all items of median difficulty. The range of item difficulties for any test will be considerable. What we can do, however, is to avoid any extremely easy or extremely difficult items. We should avoid using any item with a corrected index lower than 30 percent or higher than 70 percent. The more closely our items are concentrated around a corrected index of 50 percent, the more reliable our test will tend to be.

Many authorities in the field of testing suggest that every test should contain some very easy items to bolster the morale of the weak student and some very difficult items to test the mettle of the able student. Two observations might be made in opposition to this position. First, there is no clear evidence that either (a) students can reliably estimate the difficulty level of an item, or (b) easy items at the beginning of a test lower the level of test anxiety. Second, in the absence of such knowledge, it is better to follow a practice which we know is technically sound—that is, using only items of moderate difficulty.

DISCRIMINATION

By the *discriminating power* of a test item we mean its ability to differentiate between students of high achievement and students of low achievement. For classroom tests, we define high achievement and low achievement in terms of the scores on the test itself. We designate high achievers as those in the upper fourth or third (or some other fraction) whose answer sheets we have selected for our item analysis. Similarly, the equal number selected from the bottom of the class are designated low achievers.

All test items can be classified as either (1) positively discriminating, (2) negatively discriminating, or (3) nondiscriminating. A *positively discriminating* item is one in which the percentage of correct answers is higher in our upper group than in our lower group. A *negatively discriminating* item is one in which the reverse occurs—that is, the percentage of correct answers is higher for the lower group than for the upper group. A *nondiscriminating* item is one in which the percentage of correct answers is the same for both groups. When constructing achievement tests, our aim is to have all of our items positively discriminating. We wish to avoid or eliminate all negatively discriminating and non-discriminating items.

Why do we want only positively discriminating items in our achievement tests? We want such items because they make a positive contribution to the overall functioning of the test. Each of such items adds something to whatever it is that the test is measuring. The same cannot be said for the two other types of discrimination. A negatively discriminating item detracts from the overall functioning of the test. It is working at cross purposes with the other items. A nondiscriminating item is dead weight. It is simply taking up space in our test, contributing nothing. We would prefer to replace it with an item which is an active aid to the test.

It is possible simply to look at item-analysis data collected from our upper and lower groups and tell the nature of the discriminating power of an item. If, for example, we have ten papers in both our upper and lower groups and we see that seven people in the upper group answered an item correctly compared to five correct answers in the lower group, we know the item is positively discriminating. However, it is generally more useful to us to have a somewhat more precise estimate of the discriminating power of an item. A rather simplified index is available for this purpose. It is given by the following formula:

$$D = \frac{N_u - N_1}{N_g}, \tag{7.2}$$

where D is the index of discrimination, N_u is the number of papers in the upper group with the correct answer to the item, N_1 is the number of papers in the lower group with the correct answer to the item, and N_g is the size of the groups (both groups should always be the same size).

Let us apply this formula to the situation just mentioned where seven out of ten in the upper group and five out of ten in the lower group answered the item correctly.

$$D = \frac{7-5}{10} = \frac{+2}{10} = +0.20.$$

What do the calculated values for D tell us? We might initially suggest that D can be interpreted as sort of a crude approximation to a correlation coefficient. Most professional test publishers use some form of correlation coefficient as an index of discrimination for their test items. A discussion of these various kinds of correlation coefficients is beyond the scope of this book. Notice that the values of D adhere to the same range as a coefficient of correlation. The maximum possible positive value is +1.00; the maximum negative value is −1.00; and 0.00 indicates lack of relationship. As with relationships observed among most other natural phenomena, however, the limiting values of D are seldom achieved in practice. We can rather arbitrarily set up the following list of suggestions for obtained values of D:

Value of D	Description	Suggestions
+0.40 or higher	High positive discrimination	Keep item as is unless glaring defects are apparent
+0.20 to +0.39	Moderate positive discrimination	Revise apparent weaknesses in item; try it out again
+0.10 to +0.19	Low positive discrimination	Item should probably be discarded or else completely rewritten

Obviously, any item with an index lower than +0.10 should be discarded except in the case of the type of extenuating circumstances we shall discuss a bit later in this section.

Certain precautions should be taken in interpreting the obtained values of D. First, it should be noted that D is biased toward items of median difficulty. That is, it might appear logical to someone that an item answered correctly by eight out of ten of an upper group and by nobody in the lower group should be considered perfectly positively discriminating. It is not, of course, since such an item does not differentiate between the two persons in the upper group who missed it and the ten in the lower group who missed it. The calculated index of D, +0.80, accurately reflects this situation. Perfect positive (or perfect negative—an unlikely event) discrimination can only occur at 50 percent difficulty. This may be a virtue rather than a defect, since it will help us aim at this difficulty level in order to maximize discrimination. Second, it should also be noted that the values obtained for D are in part determined by the nature of the test itself. Since we are using total scores on the test[3] to select our upper and lower groups for item analysis, D really tells us how well that item is contributing to the total test. Now if the test consists of disparate materials, the index of discrimination for a given test item may give misleading results. Suppose, for example, we were using a 50-item multiple-choice test in geography. Of the 50 items, five called for mathematical calculations of latitude and longitude; the other 45 were knowledge items based on other materials. If the two types of achievement are not highly correlated (a distinct possibility), the indexes of discrimination for the five computation items may be low because these items are measuring factors other than those measured by the majority of the items. If this appears to be the case in a test, we should be somewhat more charitable toward low values of D for such items.

Another thing the teacher must also keep in mind is the lack of complete stability in indexes of discrimination because of the small size of the sample. The typical class has 25–40 students. We may use the papers of a maximum of 20 such students for our item analysis. It has been fairly well demonstrated that we should have about 100 in our upper and lower groups to achieve reasonable stability in our indices. Since we do not, we should expect some fluctuation each time we use an item. If the type of student and the nature of the instruction do not change greatly, we would not expect fluctuations to be too large. It is very rare that an item which has proved its worth in one test becomes negatively discriminating or nondiscriminating in another test.

[3] This is technically called an *internal* criterion, a consideration we will not develop in this book.

Before concluding this section on discrimination, we should say something about the case of the apparently relevant item which discriminates poorly. Occasionally you will find an item which is measuring an important educational outcome, which seems to be well written, but whose index of discrimination never tops the +0.20 level. What do you do in such a case? Keep the item. So long as it is positively discriminating at all it is making some contribution. Remember also that it may have a low index because it is measuring something different which the other items do not tap. In fact, it might be well to add another item or two of the same type in order to increase the contribution of this type of item to the total test score.

GATHERING ITEM-ANALYSIS DATA

You will recall that the initial step in our item-analysis procedure is to divide our class into high and low subgroups. Having divided the total group into upper and lower subgroups the task of counting the number of individuals in each of these subgroups who succeed on each of the items in the test remains. One method whereby this count may be facilitated involves the use of a *tabulation sheet*. On this sheet a row corresponding to each of the items on the test will be provided. To accommodate the tabulation of the data for the upper and lower groups separately columns will be set up on the sheet. Beginning with one of the papers in a subgroup, a tally is made on the tabulation sheet corresponding to each of the items on the test that the individual answers correctly. This procedure is followed until the correct responses of all of the individuals in both groups have been tallied. A count of the tallies will then indicate the number of individuals in each group succeeding on each of the items in the test. This is a relatively laborious process. Fortunately a somewhat easier method for obtaining this count can be devised.

This method involves the use of a typewriter. Placing the right hand in a natural position on the typewriter keyboard, the index finger will rest on the "j" key, the middle finger on the "k" key, the ring finger on the "l" key, and the little finger on the ";" key. Numbering the fingers to correspond to the response positions in a four-response multiple-choice item, we may use the typewriter to give us a sheet on which the specific response of each individual to each of the items on the test is indicated by a code symbol. To prepare this sheet we insert a blank piece of paper in the typewriter, and, beginning with the first individual in one of the groups, we note in turn his response to each of the items on the test and depress the finger that corresponds to that response. When we have completed the responses of the first individual, we return the carriage and begin a second row with the responses of the second individual. We continue in this manner until we have completed the responses of all the individuals in both groups. The result is a data sheet similar to the one shown in Fig. 7.3. In case an item has been omitted, the "o" key on the typewriter is depressed. In case the multiple-choice item has five responses, the little finger is put to double service and the "¢" sign on the typewriter is used to represent a fifth response.

On the data sheet obtained through the use of this method each row corresponds to the responses of one individual to the different items on the test. It is now a relatively simple matter to count the number of individuals in each group selecting each response to each item. For example, on the data sheet provided in Fig. 7.3, in the first column of figures for the upper group we will notice that there are two "j's". This means that on the first item of this test two individuals in the upper group selected the first response. In this same column for the upper group we notice that there are two "k's". This indicates that two individuals in this group selected the second response for the first item. Similarly, we may note that 15 individuals in the upper group selected the third response to the first item and one individual in this group selected the fourth response. Since the "¢" sign does not appear, no individual in the upper group selected the fifth response to the first item on the test. Proceeding in a similar manner for the lower group, we may obtain the number of individuals selecting each response to

Figure 7.3 Coded item count for sample test.

```
Upper group  1klk1;;1¢jkj1ll    1kk1ll;11j1;;k;    k;kk1;;1k;¢
             1kllj;;k¢llj1;1    kkk1ll;;1j1;1;;    k¢kk1;;1klk
             1klk1;;k¢llj1ll    llk1ll;1ll;;1j;    k;1k1;;1k;k
             1;1klj;k¢llj1ll    1kk1ll;1llj1l;;    ;1;k1;;1k;k
             j;1kj;;k¢j1j;j1    1kk1ll;11j;;1k;    k;;k1;j1klk1k
             1;1kl;;;kj1j1ll    1kk1ll;1ll;;1j¢    k;kk1;;jk;k
             ;klk1;;k¢;1j1kl    1kk1ll;1ll;;1k¢    k;kk1;;1k;k
             j;1kl;;¢¢llj;j1    1kk1llk1lj1;1;;    k¢;1k;kjk1k
             1;1klj;k¢;1j;;1    1kk1ll;1lk;;1l;    k;;k1;;kk1k
             1klk1;;;¢llj1kl    kkk1ll;;1;j;1;;    k1;k1;;1k1k
             1kl¢1;;;¢llj1;1    1kk1ll;;11k1;1;    k;kk1;j1kl¢
             k;1;j;;¢¢llljkll   1kk;11;1ll;;1;;    k11k1;;1klk
             1kl;1lk;¢lljklk    1kk1ll;1ll1;1;;    k;;k1;;kk1k
             1klkj;;k¢lljkll    llk1ll;1ll;11k;    k;1k1;;1k;k
             1klkj;;¢¢llj1ll    k;k1ll;1ll;11k;    k;;k1;;1k;k
             1;lll;;k¢llj1;k    1;k1j1;1llj;1j;    k¢1k1;k1k;;
             1kllj1;¢¢lljkll    1kk1ll;1llj;1k;    k;;k1;;1k;¢
             1klkj;kk¢llj;;1    1kk1j1;;1l;;1k;    k;kk1;;1k;k
             k;1;1j;;¢llj1ll    1kk1ll;;1ll;1k¢    k;;j1;k1k1k
             1kl¢1;k;¢llj1ll    1kk;11;;1j;11;;    k;1j1;;1k;k


Lower group  jklk1;j;¢llj1k1    1kkk11;1111;1jk    k¢kk1;;11;k
             kk1ll;;k¢lljk1l    llk;11;1111;1k¢    k;;k1;;kk;k
             1kllj;kk¢llj1ll    llk;11;111j11k¢    k;kk1;;1kjk
             jklk1kk;¢11j1k;    1jk;k;111111;;     k;kk1;;1kl¢
             1kllj;;¢¢lljk;1    llk1k1;111j;1k;    k;kk1;k1k1k
             1kll1;;;¢j1j1;1    llk1j1;;1jj;1k¢    k;;k1;k1k1k
             1;lll;;;¢j1j;j1    1kk;j1;;1j¢;1k;    k;jk11;kk1k
             1;1klk;¢¢lll jjll  1kk1ll;1kkj;1k;    k1;j1;k1k;k
             k;lll;;;¢jljkll    11k;;11;;11;;1;;   k;;k11;1k1k
             1klkj1kl¢¢l1j1ll   1jk1ll;;11;11k¢    k;kk1;j1k1k
             1kl;1kk1¢j1jk1j    1kk1j1;;1j1;;j;    k;;k;;;kk;k
             1klk1;;;¢llj;k1    1kk1¢1k;11;;1k;    j1;k1;;1kjk
             ¢;1;1;k¢¢¢j1j1ll   1kk;11k;111;1k;    k;;k1;jkk;k
             j¢1;lk;¢¢llj1ll    llk1k1;;11;11k1    k;;k1;klk1k
             ¢;lllk;;¢lljkj1    k1kj111;1j;k;j;    k;kk1;k;k1k
             j¢1kl;;;¢ll1j;;k   11k1¢1¢llkj;1;¢    k;1k1k;kj1¢
             1;1j1;kk¢jljk;1    1kk1k1;;11;11k;    k¢;k11jkk;k
             jk1;1;;;¢;1j1;1    1kkj11;;111;1k¢    kk;j11;kk;k
             1¢1;1;k;¢j1lk;1    1kk111k;1j;;1k¢    k1;k1;j1k;k
             jklk1;;;¢lljk;1    11k;¢1k;11;j1k¢    k;;k1;j¢k1k


Answer       1;1k1;;k¢llj1ll    1kk1ll;11j1;1;;    k;kk1;;1k1;
```

the first item. The data for the first item on this test as obtained from
Fig. 7.3 is summarized in Table 7.1.

**TABLE 7.1   FREQUENCY OF RESPONSES
TO ITEM 1 ON SAMPLE TEST.**

Response	Group	
	Upper	Lower
1	2	6
2	2	2
3	15	10
4	1	0
5	0	2
Omit	0	0

For each of the items on the test we can obtain a summary similar to
Table 7.1. Noting that the answer to the first item on this test is the
third response we can see that 15 individuals in the upper group and 10
individuals in the lower group succeeded on this item. The number of
individuals in the groups succeeding on the item is therefore 25. Since
40 students took this test and since all of the students attempted this
item, we will express 25, the number of students succeeding on the
item, as a percent of 40 to obtain the index of difficulty. Rounding to
the nearest percent the index of difficulty for this item is 63 percent.
To obtain the index of discrimination for this item we will subtract
from the number of individuals succeeding in the upper group the
number of individuals succeeding in the lower group; that is, 15 – 10.
This difference is five and its sign is positive. Dividing the positive 5
by the maximum possible difference between the two groups, 20,
we obtain a value for D of +0.25.

USING ITEM-ANALYSIS DATA TO REVISE TEST ITEMS

Once we have accumulated our item-analysis data, it is sometimes
possible to make use of the information in order to revise a weak item.

Items, so revised, can be used at a later time, and if the revision has been successful, the item may function well in the new test. This type of revision works best with multiple-choice items, although it can also be used with matching and classification items. Let us see how it works.

In a multiple-choice item, it is possible to determine not only whether the item itself is functioning properly but also whether each of the responses is functioning as we would like. Figure 7.4 shows how item-analysis data should look for a properly functioning multiple-choice item. Note that each of the responses is positively discriminating. Response number 2, the answer, is functioning well. Seven students in the upper group chose it; only three in the lower group picked it. What is also important, the incorrect responses or distractors are also working well. In the case of distractors, we want students in the lower group to pick these responses with a frequency greater than that of students in the upper group. This has happened for all of the distractors in our item. Such an item can be retained and used again just as it is.

In Fig. 7.5, we present a picture of an item which is just the reverse. This item has a number of faults. First, we can see that the item is slightly negatively discriminating. Only three persons in the upper group picked response number 4, the answer; four in the lower group picked it. Response number 1 is also negatively discriminating; response

Figure 7.4   Item-analysis data for a properly functioning multiple-choice item.

Date

Diff.	50%	
Disc.	+0.40	
Response	U	L
1	1	2
* 2	7	3
3	1	3
4	1	2
5	—	—
Omit	—	—

Figure 7.5   Item-analysis data for an improperly functioning multiple-choice item.

Date

Response	U	L
Diff.	35%	
Disc.	−0.10	
1	5	4
2	2	2
3	0	0
* 4	3	4
5		
Omit		

number 2 is nondiscriminating. Response number 3 appears to be an implausible distractor since nobody chose it.

What can be done about an item such as the one in Fig. 7.5? First of all, there is obviously something about response number 1 which makes it too attractive. Perhaps it is somewhat ambiguous. The item-analysis data will not tell us exactly what is wrong. They will only tell us that *something* is wrong with the response. We must try to figure out what it is and change the response accordingly. It is also obvious that something is wrong with response number 3; nobody picks it. It is nonfunctional in the item. We had best attempt to replace it with a more plausible distractor. If we change these two responses, we may not have to tamper with the other two. If we revise response number 1, some of our upper group who were misled by it may now choose response 4, the answer. Response number 2 is functioning, and the fact that it is nondiscriminating at this particular administration may be an artifact of the small sample. Perhaps we can just leave it alone and see how it works next time.

Through the type of analysis demonstrated here, we can take our defective items, particularly multiple-choice items, and salvage them for further use. Some items, of course, will not be worth saving. As we grow more proficient at item writing, these should occur less frequently.

MAKING AND USING ITEM FILES

The major purpose of item analysis is to ensure that items are functioning properly so they may be used again at some future time. If items are to be used again, provisions must be made for this.

First of all, provision must be made for a certain amount of test security. Items to be used again cannot be allowed to circulate freely among students. Obviously, this would spoil their effectiveness as measuring devices. This means that tests must not come into the possession of students. It does not mean that the teacher cannot hand the test back to students and discuss the items and their answers in class. It does mean, however, that the tests must be collected after the discussion is finished. This practice bothers many teachers. They feel that the students will learn more if they are allowed to keep the test after the discussion. This presumed increment of learning has never been demonstrated to occur, and logic might dictate that the reverse would happen. Few students are zealously interested in the items of tests after the excitement of taking it has expired. Even if they were, it might not be a good way to learn because a test is, after all, only a sample of all items which might have gone into it. Concentration on the particular set of items comprising this sample might restrict the student from a proper exposure to other elements in the entire universe of potential items. So it is best to keep your achievement tests relatively secure. An easy way to do this is to number each test booklet so you know that it has been returned.

Unless a test happens to be a particularly good one with no defective items, it is unlikely that you will wish to use it again in exactly the same form. What you need is some method of keeping track of the individual items in the test and the item-analysis data for those items. The usual way of doing this is to start a test-item file. An example of a card for such a file is shown in Fig. 7.6. Note that this card has room at the bottom for the test item. It may be typed on the card, or the item may be cut out of a copy of the test and stapled to the card. It also has

Figure 7.6   Item-analysis card.

Class	Date			Date			Date			Date		
	Diff.			Diff.			Diff.			Diff.		
	Disc.			Disc.			Disc.			Disc.		
	Response	U	L	Response	U	L	Response	U	L	Response	U	L
	1			1			1			1		
	2			2			2			2		
	3			3			3			3		
	4			4			4			4		
	5			5			5			5		
	Omit			Omit			Omit			Omit		

a place to record the class in which the item was used and the dates of use. Space is provided for item analysis data from four administrations of the item. With four administrations, you can begin to achieve reasonably stable item statistics.

Item files can be maintained in whatever manner is most efficient for the person using them. Most teachers like to use a card file with identification dividers separating the cards into sections. These sections are usually appropriate topic divisions of the subject matter. Within the divisions, each card may be cross-classified by objective and by content. Thus, for example, within a division labeled "Latitude and Longitude," a teacher might have an item cross-classified as "calculation—time" which looks like this:

How long does it take the earth to rotate a distance of $10°$ of longitude?

a. 30 min.

b. 40 min.

c. 60 min.

d. 90 min.

The most important feature of an item file is that it allows the teacher to make up a new examination to fit a table of specifications. The items are there. All the teacher needs to do is to select the type of item called for by the specifications. Once the item file has been built to a reasonable length, the number of items in most cross-classification categories will have increased to the point where a given item need not be used each time a new test is built. This will help to maintain test security. The item file will also make it possible to construct parallel forms of a test if the teacher desires to do so. Where two items testing the same item idea are available, one can be assigned randomly to one form of the test and the other to the second, parallel form.

The practice of building and maintaining an item file can be very helpful to a teacher. Once such a file is reasonably complete, the labor of constructing new examinations is greatly reduced. The little added effort involved will certainly pay big dividends to any teacher willing to implement the necessary procedures.

REMINDER

It should be remembered that the techniques of item analysis described in this chapter are relevant only to tests of relative achievement. The purpose of such tests is to place students as accurately as possible along a continuum of achievement. When mastery tests are employed, the concepts of difficulty and discrimination lose most of their significance. The items from such tests would typically be much easier (average index of 85–90 percent), and indexes of discrimination, if calculated at all, would be very low. Teachers employing both types of tests should remember these differences.

8
STANDARDIZED
TESTS

In evaluating the educational achievement of his pupils, the teacher will usually rely on tests and observational techniques of his own devising rather than on published standardized tests. This is as it must be since available standardized tests will rarely measure fully the specific objectives of instruction of the teacher. When, however, the objectives that the test measures coincide with those of the teacher, a standardized test provides useful information that cannot be obtained from teacher-made devices. This information is given by the *norms* which accompany the standardized test and which permit the interpretation of scores in comparison to larger and hopefully more representative groups than are available in any classroom or school.

THE STANDARDIZATION PROCEDURE

When a standardized test is being prepared, the first step is to determine the objectives which the test is to measure. This leads to the establishment of a table of specifications. Items are then written to fit the table. These activities are generally carried on by a number of specialists in the subject-matter field and in test construction. More items than are planned for the final form (or forms) of the test are usually prepared. From these items preliminary forms of the test are assembled. Since a standardized test is designed to be administered in a variety of locations but under as standard conditions as possible, specific, detailed instructions for administration are also prepared.

The preliminary forms of the test are then administered to reasonably large samples of students comparable to those with whom the test is designed to be used. The purpose of this administration is to permit item-analysis data to be obtained. On the basis of these data and the table of specifications, items are selected for inclusion in the final form(s) of the test.

The final form is then administered to a different, large sample of students. The norm tables are prepared on the basis of the scores from this administration. One or more of three basic types of norms are computed. These types—percentile ranks, age and grade equivalent scores, and standard scores—will be treated in more detail in Chapter 9. Here it is only necessary to note that norms provide a basis for comparing individual and group performances to the performance of the norming sample.

THE SELECTION OF TEST CONTENT

As has been indicated, the first concern in the preparation of a standardized achievement test is the specification of the objectives of instruction that the test is to measure. A special problem is presented in this respect by the fact that standardized tests are designed to be used in a variety of different schools, and the specific objectives for particular courses may vary from school to school. One approach to a solution of this problem is to collect from different schools information about such things as statements of objectives, courses of study, and textbooks used. From these data, an attempt is made to determine objectives and course content which are common to many, if not most, of the schools. This may be referred to as the *common-curriculum* approach. Its principal limitation, of course, comes from the fact that for certain subject-matter areas there may be little common content among the courses in the various schools. In some areas—mathematics, for example—courses in different schools may be quite similar; in other areas—for example, literature—the specific course content may vary widely. If such tests are required, teachers tend minimally to concentrate their instruction on the topics covered by the test. In areas such as literature where the specific content may reasonably differ extremely, the use of standardized tests of the common curriculum type may well discourage the most innovative and creative teachers.

A second approach to the selection of content for standardized achievement tests does not concern itself directly with what *is* being taught in the schools. Rather it concentrates on those objectives of instruction which it is agreed *should* be taught in all schools regardless of the particular structure and content of the curriculum. These objectives tend to define those abilities of students which have been identified as the basic skills; and this approach to determining test content may be referred to as the *basic-skills* approach. Among the basic skills certainly are reading, computation, and reasoning with numbers, the use of the English language, and spelling. Map and graph-reading ability and the ability to use the dictionary and other standard reference sources may also be included. Most of the standardized achievement tests on the market today are basic skills tests.

SURVEY AND DIAGNOSTIC TESTS

Most standardized achievement tests are designed to give an indication of how far the student has progressed toward the accomplishment of the specific objectives measured by the test. These objectives, however, are grouped in broad categories. A reading comprehension test, for example, will give an assessment of how well the student comprehends written material. It will identify students who are having relative difficulty in this area, but it will not identify the causes of reading disability. Such *survey* tests serve a useful function, but in order to help the student with a disability, the teacher will need to analyze the specific nature of the difficulty and the causes for the trouble. *Diagnostic* tests are designed to assist in this process. The diagnostic test attempts to break a complex skill like reading into related parts, such as word and letter recognition, and to provide separate measures of these subskills.

Attempts have been made to construct tests to serve both the survey and the diagnostic purposes. In general, these attempts have not been successful. Each of the various parts of a diagnostic test must be made reasonably long in order to assure reasonable reliability. If the test is short enough for practical use as a survey device, the diagnostic subscores are of questionable reliability; if the subtests are long enough to assure reasonable reliability, the whole test is too long for practical use with all students. Further, it may be argued that there is little point in diagnosing the nature of a disability unless that disability is known to exist. If administered at all, diagnostic tests are usually reserved for those students who, on the basis of a survey test, have been identified as having possible learning disabilities. Frequently, the competent teacher can, through his own tests and informal observations, adequately identify his pupils' sources of difficulty without the use of standardized diagnostic tests.

SOURCES OF INFORMATION ABOUT STANDARDIZED TESTS

With the large number of standardized tests available, the problem of selecting a particular test or battery for use in the schools may be a formidable one. While the final decision should not be made without direct consideration of the test and its manual, it is desirable to obtain information on the basis of which the field can be narrowed to a reasonable number.

The best and most complete source of preliminary information about standardized tests is from the *Mental Measurement Yearbooks*, edited by Oscar K. Buros. These books provide a comprehensive, if not exhaustive, list of psychological and educational tests available at the date of publication of the yearbook. In addition, critical reviews of the tests are provided. These reviews are written by authorities who have no connection with the particular test. An extensive bibliography of research and reviews related to the test is also given. Unfortunately the "yearbooks" are not published yearly; the Sixth Yearbook, which is the latest, was published in 1965. Information is, therefore, not available from this source for tests published or revised since that date.

Information about tests may also be obtained from the periodic reviews carried in journals. These are particularly helpful with respect to recently published tests. Among the most useful are the *Journal of Educational Measurement*, the *Journal of Counseling Psychology*, and the *Personnel and Guidance Journal*.

When the number of tests under consideration has been narrowed to a few, specimen sets of test materials should be obtained from the publishers. These sets usually contain a copy of the test, scoring keys, a sample answer sheet, the manual for administration, and frequently a technical manual. Specimen sets are available at nominal cost. Because test publishers wish to control the distribution of materials to assure test security, orders for specimen sets or any other material should be written on school letterhead stationery.

The manuals for the test generally give a description of the test, the procedures used in its development, tables of norms, and a description of the norming sample. Since the norms describe test performance relative to the group on which those norms were based, it is important that the test user is aware of the nature of the norming sample. Reports of reliability studies may also be included in the manuals together with validity studies if such have been made. It should be remembered, however, that empirical studies of the validity of achievement tests may be difficult, if not impossible, because of the lack of an adequate, outside criterion.

Undoubtedly the most useful information for the selection of a standardized achievement test can be obtained from an examination of the test questions themselves. This may be the only way in which an adequate judgment of the relevance of the test to the particular school situation can be made.

SUGGESTIONS AND PRECAUTIONS IN THE USE OF STANDARDIZED TESTS

The principal advantage of standardized tests derives from the norms that they provide to assist the teacher in the interpretation of scores. If these norms are to have the intended meaning, certain suggestions must be followed and certain precautions kept in mind.

1. Follow explicitly the directions for administering the test. If any condition is introduced into the test situation which was not present when the test was administered to the norming sample, it may have an influence on the scores obtained. Those scores are then not directly comparable to scores obtained under different conditions, and the meaning of the norms is questionable.

2. Know the nature of the norming sample. School districts frequently find that their pupils consistently perform, on the average, above (or below) the average on the norms. This may, of course, reflect conditions in the instructional program of the schools in the district over which the school has little control.

3. If possible, develop local norms. Because of the variation in pupils from one locale to another, local norms can provide useful information both for the interpretation of individual scores and for describing the local population of students. In larger school systems, reasonably reliable norms can be obtained from a single, systemwide administration of a test. In smaller systems when the same test is used

over a number of years, data can be accumulated over those years to provide an adequate base for computing local norms.

4. Remember that norms describe how students *do* perform; they do not describe how students *can* or *should* perform. Judgments about whether a given student is performing as well as he *should* must take into account all of the pertinent information of which the teacher is aware. Knowing how he *does* perform, however, is an essential part of that pertinent information.

5. Remember that no test, including standardized tests, gives perfectly reliable scores. There seems to be a tendency for some users of standardized tests to assume that the norming process somehow improves the quality of the scores, that the norms somehow provide more reliable assessments of achievement. This is simply not true. No statistical procedure can improve the quality of the data on which it is based. If anything, converted scores derived from norm tables may be less reliable than the raw scores on which they are based. The fact that the norms are based on a sample of students introduces another potential source of error, namely, that the sample, systematically or by chance, does not represent the population from which it is drawn. This precaution should not be carried too far. While the scores from standardized tests are not perfectly reliable, they tend to be more reliable than those from most teacher-made tests because of the care taken in the preparation and selection of test items.

9
STATISTICAL
TREATMENT
OF
TEST SCORES

Having constructed, administered, and scored a test, the teacher is faced with the problem of what to do with the results. These results are usually in the form of numbers. Each number represents the number of items a student has answered correctly. What is the teacher to do with these numbers? The purpose of this chapter is to answer that question.

First of all, let us be clear about the "meaning" of the number with which we are dealing. The number itself has little intrinsic meaning other than that described in the previous paragraph, that is, simply the number of items answered correctly on the test. This bit of knowledge really tells us very little about the number. If we know that Johnny received a score of 30 on a history test, exactly what do we know that goes beyond this simple datum? Nothing. In order to give meaning to this number, we have to interpret it as it stands *in relation* to other numbers.

One suggestion is that we interpret this number in relation to the number of items on the test. If, in our example, the history test contained 50 items, Johnny would have answered 60 percent of them correctly. In past years, many teachers were willing to accept such a relational statement as one carrying intrinsic meaning. The so-called *absolute system* of grading was based upon the assumption that such percentages could be used as relatively invariant indices of achievement. A percentage of 85 was considered to have the same meaning whether it was derived from different tests, in different subjects, or on different students. We now recognize, of course, that a percentage score is relative to the difficulty of the test. A percentage of 85 might actually be a very low score if the test were extremely easy. Conversely, if the test were difficult, 85 percent might represent outstanding achievement. Because of this ambiguity in meaning, we seldom interpret test scores in this fashion, except in the case of mastery tests. For the achievement test, we prefer a different relational meaning.

The most useful approach to the interpretation of achievement test scores is to interpret them in relation to each other. The major reason for this approach is that it avoids the ambiguity inherent in the percentage approach described in the previous paragraph. Since we cannot accurately predict the difficulty of test items or of tests prior to their administration, we know that a percentage score will not possess invariant meaning. On the other hand, an interpretation which fixes the position of a test score within its own set of scores will have invariant meaning so long as we do not go outside the set. In addition, we can bring to bear on such scores that branch of mathematics known as *descriptive statistics*.[1] This, we shall find, is a great advantage.

Perhaps we should explain the use of the word "descriptive" in relation to statistics and test scores. Once a teacher has obtained a set of

---

[1] The field of statistics is generally divided into two main branches, descriptive and inferential. We shall deal only with the former in this book.

test scores, we could legitimately ask him to "describe" these scores to us. He could attempt a verbal description by saying, for example, that there seemed to be a great many of them; some were larger than others; some impressed him and some distressed him; some were more beautiful than others. We might go away with a heightened respect for our teacher's esthetic sensitivity to numbers but with little in the way of hard information. Because of the inadequacies of verbal description, we prefer numerical description of test scores. Numerical descriptions have the advantages of succinctness, clarity, and nonemotionality.[2] Descriptive statistics contains many procedures which we can apply to describe numerically, in many different ways, our set of test scores.

FREQUENCY DISTRIBUTIONS

One of the first tasks of the teacher is to bring some order out of the random array of test scores as they come off the answer sheets or test booklets. The simplest and most obvious step is to arrange the scores in order of magnitude. We usually do this by placing the largest scores on top and the smallest ones on the bottom.[3] Even this simple procedure adds a great deal of meaning to the individual test scores. This simple order relationship is basic to most of our future calculations. The effect of this type of treatment is illustrated in Figs. 9.1 and 9.2. Figure 9.1 contains a set of unordered scores derived from a 50-item test of American history. Figure 9.2 shows the same scores arranged in rank order. Note the increase in meaning for each score as a result of this manipulation.

The arrangement of the scores in Fig. 9.2 is called a *rank-order* distribution. For the calculation of many of the descriptive statistics we

[2] There are some who would dispute the accuracy of this last term. The numerical description 38-24-36 has been known to bring smiles to the lips of many members of an adult population.

[3] There is no particularly good reason why the reverse procedure should not be employed. Other professions, notably economists, place the smallest values on top and the largest values on the bottom. No doubt this difference in procedure reflects a basic personality difference between economists and psychologists.

EDUCATIONAL MEASUREMENT AND EVALUATION

Figure 9.1 Scores of 25 students on a 50-item American history test.

20	18	38	19	37
33	30	26	31	23
28	40	15	42	30
45	31	29	29	26
29	24	35	35 —	32

Figure 9.2 Scores of 25 students on a 50-item American history test arranged in order of rank.

Scores
45
42
40
38
37
35
35
33
32
31
31
30
30
29
29
29
28
26
26
24
23
20
19
18
15

plan to present in this chapter, it is possible to work with test scores arranged in this manner. For the beginner, however, it is inadvisable to do so because he is likely to make mistakes in calculations. It is also inadvisable because the form of presentation used in Fig. 9.2 may give a misleading impression about the scores. It would appear, for example, that the difference between the top score of 45 and the next score of 42 was no greater or of no more significance than the difference between any two other contiguous scores, say, 30 and 29. This, obviously, is not the case. To avoid such errors and misleading impressions we will frequently recast our scores in a form known as a *simple frequency distribution*, sometimes called merely a *frequency distribution.*

To make a simple frequency distribution we set up a column of numbers under the heading "Score." The top number in this column is equal to our highest score; the bottom number is equal to our lowest score. We include all possible score values between these two limiting values. Then we set up beside our score column another column labeled "Tallies." In this column we place a tally mark to the right of the appropriate score value for each score in our set of test scores. Next, we count all the tallies for each score value and place the result in a column labeled "Frequency" or more commonly, simply "*f.*" This process is illustrated for our 25 test scores in Fig. 9.3. The tallying process is considered an intermediate step toward the construction of a frequency distribution. Technically, the frequency distribution itself consists of only the two columns, "Score" and *f.*

As in the case of the rank-order distribution, it is possible to work directly from a simple frequency distribution in calculating our statistics. We shall demonstrate these procedures later in this chapter. In some situations and for some purposes, however, we prefer to present our scores in still a different form, a form which we call the *grouped frequency distribution*. A simple frequency distribution is changed to a grouped frequency distribution by combining the values in the "Score" column into *intervals*. Each interval contains a number of score values rather than the single score value found in the simple frequency distribution. Why do we combine the scores into intervals? There are basi-

Figure 9.3 Procedure for constructing a simple frequency distribution.

Score	Tallies	f	Score	Tallies	f
45	/	1	30	/ /	2
44		0	29	/ / /	3
43		0	28	/	1
42	/	1	27		0
41		0	26	/ /	2
40	/	1	25		0
39		0	24	/	1
38	/	1	23	/	1
37	/	1	22		0
36		0	21		0
35	/ /	2	20	/	1
34		0	19	/	1
33	/	1	18	/	1
32	/	1	17		0
31	/ /	2	16		0
			15	/	1

cally two reasons for this. First, the resulting format frequently gives a better picture of the manner in which the scores from the test are distributed, particularly if the range of scores is a large one. If we look at Fig. 9.3, we can see that the scores are "strung out" over a range of 30 points, and that it is difficult to get a mental image of the regions of concentration of the scores. Grouping the scores will make it easier for us to "see" the distribution. Second, grouping will make our calculations somewhat less laborious. This saving in effort will not be too great for small numbers of scores, but as the number of scores increases in magnitude, the saving will be considerable.

If we propose to group our scores into intervals, the obvious question is: How do we decide upon the *size* of each interval, that is, the number of score values which will be included in each interval? The answer to this question is a rather arbitrary one. From experience we have learned that grouped frequency distributions work best if they contain somewhere between 10 and 20 intervals. The decision concerning the number of intervals to use is another example of the application of the

Scylla-Charybdis principle. If we use too many intervals, we do not noticeably decrease the extent of our labors in calculation. If we use too few intervals, we increase the degree of distortion imposed on our raw data and increase the amount of error in our statistics. Error would be defined here as the difference in values for a statistic (such as a mean) calculated from scores when arranged in a simple frequency distribution and from the same scores when arranged in a grouped frequency distribution. This error occurs because, as we shall see, we lose the identity of the individual scores when we group them into intervals. Since we have arbitrarily decided that we wish to use somewhere between 10 and 20 intervals, we take our range of scores (the difference between the highest and lowest score) and divide it by both of these figures. The range of scores in our distribution is 30 (45-15), so dividing by 10 gives us 3, and dividing by 20 gives us 1.5. We compare these results with a list of *preferred* sizes of intervals. These preferred sizes are 2, 3, 5, 7, 10, or any higher multiple of 5. In most cases, with the exceptions of 2 and 10, we prefer an odd number as the size of our interval because the midpoint of the interval will then be a whole number. As we shall see later, this consideration will be important to us. In the case of our distribution of scores, therefore, we shall choose 3 as the size of the interval.

Having selected the size of interval we plan to use, we must next decide which shall be the three scores that constitute each interval. Again, our procedure for doing this is an arbitrary one. We simply say that the lowest score in the interval shall be a multiple of the size of the interval. We then begin with our highest score and write our interval so that the highest score is included. In our distribution, the highest score is 45 which is itself a multiple of three. Our top interval would include scores of 45, 46, and 47, which we usually write simply as 45-47. We have no scores of 46 or 47 in our distribution, but that is immaterial so far as writing our intervals is concerned. We then proceed to write intervals down to the place where the lowest score is incorporated into the bottom interval. Then we count the number of scores falling within each interval and enter that number in the frequency column. The result will look like Fig. 9.4 which is a grouped frequency distribution of our 25 test scores. Note that when the scores are placed in a grouped frequency distribution, we can tell something about the *shape* of the distribution. This distribution appears roughly symmetrical except for the distortion introduced by the three scores in the interval 18–20. It is the type of distribution we might expect to get in regular classroom testing.

In the remaining sections of this chapter, we shall discuss the calculations of various descriptive statistics from both simple and grouped frequency distribution.

Figure 9.4   Grouped frequency distribution.

Interval	f
45–47	1
42–44	1
39–41	1
36–38	2
33–35	3
30–32	5
27–29	4
24–26	3
21–23	1
18–20	3
15–17	1

GRAPHICAL REPRESENTATIONS OF FREQUENCY DISTRIBUTIONS

Sometimes, in order to get a better picture of the manner in which a set of test scores is distributed, it is to our advantage to represent these scores in graphical form. Although there are a number of such types of graphical representation, we shall discuss only two here: (1) the *histogram* or *bar graph*, and (2) the *frequency polygon* or *line graph*.

Histogram. A histogram constructed from the scores in our grouped frequency distribution is presented in Fig. 9.5. Let us explain how this histogram was constructed and what it means.

A histogram is constructed by laying off a pair of coordinates or axes. On the horizontal or X axis (abscissa) we lay off an appropriate scale corresponding to the scores on our test. Normally, this scale runs from slightly below our lowest score to slightly above our highest score. On the vertical or Y axis (ordinate) we lay off a frequency scale. As a general rule of thumb (for esthetic reasons) we make the Y axis about two-thirds to three-fourths as long as the X axis. We divide the Y axis into equal units representing frequencies. The highest value on the Y axis will be equal to our highest frequency.

Having laid off our coordinates in this fashion, the next step is to construct the *bars* that form the basis of our histogram. Beginning with the bottom interval of our grouped frequency distribution, we draw a straight line at the level of the appropriate frequency along the complete length of each interval. For example, for our bottom interval

Figure 9.5 Histogram.

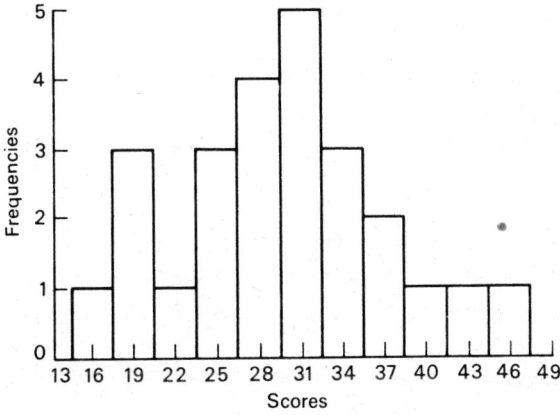

15-17, we would draw a line at the level of one frequency between the two points 14.5 and 17.5 on our score scale. Then we would connect this line with the bottom of our scale at the points 14.5 and 17.5.

Perhaps a word of explanation is in order here about the use of the points 14.5 and 17.5. Why do we use these instead of 15 and 17? We refer to the former pair of points as the *real* limits of the interval and the latter pair as the *integral* limits of the interval. The real limits are so-called because we are dealing with continuous variables. If you will re-call our discussion in the first chapter of this book, you will remember that we defined what we meant by a continuous variable. You may re-call that in continuous variation, the units of measurement may be in-finitely subdivided and that the numbers identifying such units are to be considered intervals rather than points. For example, the number 15, which is the lowest integral limit of our lowest interval, actually represents an interval extending from the point 14.5 to the point 15.5. Similarly, 17, which is the upper integral limit of the same interval, represents an interval extending from 16.5-17.5. Our interval, then, really extends from the lower limit of 15, which is 14.5, to the upper limit of 17, which is 17.5. The real limits of the interval 15-17 are thus 14.5-17.5.

We complete our histogram by following the same procedure for each interval. The result of this procedure is a bar graph where the total area of the graph represents the total number of scores on our test, and the area of each bar is proportional to the frequency within that interval. The major purpose of such a graph is, of course, to give us a visual image of the distribution.

Frequency polygon. A frequency polygon serves much the same pur-pose as a histogram, that is, to provide a visual image of the shape of a distribution of scores. It is somewhat easier to construct than a histo-gram.

To make a frequency polygon, we begin with a pair of axes similar to those used in constructing a histogram. In fact, we frequently superimpose a frequency polygon on a histogram. For purposes of illustration, however, we shall construct the two separately.

Figure 9.6 illustrates a frequency polygon constructed from the data in our grouped frequency distribution. Notice that the coordinates have been constructed in the same way and labeled exactly the same as in the histogram. In the frequency polygon, instead of drawing a line at the appropriate frequency along the length of each interval, we simply place a dot at the midpoint of that interval. For our lowest interval, for example, we place a dot at a frequency value of one, immediately above the point 16 on our score scale. Similarly, we place dots at the appropriate frequency levels above the score points 19, 22, 25, 28, 31, 34, 37, 40, 43, and 46. Note that we also place a dot at zero frequency at the two points 13 and 49. This is to *complete* the frequency polygon, that is, bring it back to the base line. Having located the dots properly, we connect consecutive dots with straight lines. The result is a line graph such as that appearing in Fig. 9.6.

The *curves* that we frequently employ to demonstrate certain types

Figure 9.6   Frequency polygon.

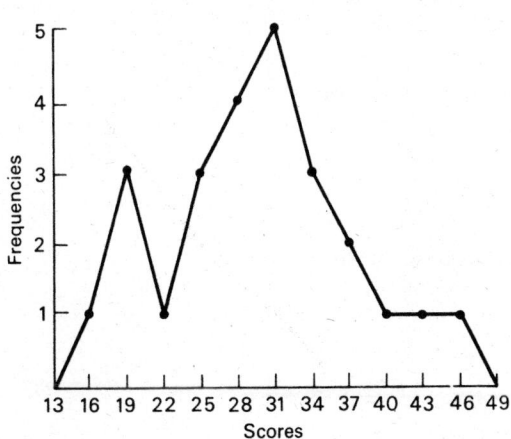

of distributions, for example, a positively skewed distribution, are nothing more than *smoothed* frequency polygons. A frequency polygon such as that presented in Fig. 9.6 has a rather jagged and irregular appearance. Such irregularities might detract from the main impression we are trying to create when we talk about a certain "type" of distribution. We usually represent such types of distributions in the abstract by ignoring the irregularities we find in actual distributions and drawing a general model such as the model of a positively skewed distribution found in Fig. 9.7. Notice that in such general models, we typically do not include the frequency scale along the ordinate. This scale is simply understood.

MEASURES OF CENTRAL TENDENCY

The use of graphs such as histograms and frequency polygons allows us to present a visual description of a set of test scores. It is also possible to describe the same set of test scores with certain numerical indices. The most common of such indices are those we call (1) measures of central tendency, and (2) measures of variability. We shall describe measures of central tendency in this section and measures of variability in the next.

A *measure of central tendency* (also called an *average*) is a numerical index derived from a set of scores whose function it is to represent those scores. In other words, it is a *representative* measure. If, for example, another teacher were to ask you how your class did on a cer-

Figure 9.7   A positively skewed distribution.

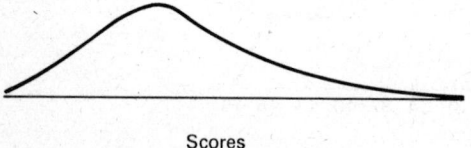

Scores

tain test, how would you reply? You might say, "Not too well," or make some other evaluative comment, or you might say that the median score was 30. If you choose the latter approach, you are employing descriptive statistics, and you are selecting a numerical value (30—the median) to represent the general performance level of the class. Notice that the value selected is one near the central part of the distribution. We would not normally consider reporting a high or a low score as being representative of the class. Because values near the middle of a distribution are most representative, we prefer these to values from any other portion of the distribution. The general expression applied to such representative values is "measure of central tendency." We shall discuss three such measures: (1) the *mode*, (2) the *median*, and (3) the *mean*.

The mode. The mode is the simplest of the measures of central tendency. In a simple frequency distribution, the mode is defined as the score value having the highest frequency. In a grouped frequency distribution, it is defined as the midpoint of the interval having the highest frequency. If we look back at Fig. 9.3, we see that the mode is equal to 29 because this score occurs three times while no other score occurs more than twice. When the same scores are placed in a grouped frequency distribution, as in Fig. 9.4, the mode now becomes 31, the midpoint of the interval 30–32, because the frequency for this interval is five, the highest frequency in the distribution.

This kind of instability in the mode is one of its major weaknesses as a measure of central tendency. As we shall see shortly, neither the median nor the mean will be affected this much by calculating from a grouped frequency distribution rather than from a simple frequency distribution.

Another difficulty with the mode is that it may have more than one value. If we have two scores that occur with equal frequency or if we have two intervals with equal frequency, we have what is known as a *bimodal* distribution. It is also possible to have three or more modes in a *multimodal* distribution. In such cases, the mode is practically useless as a measure of central tendency.

The big advantage of the mode is that no calculations are involved in arriving at its value. We can simply look at a distribution of scores and tell the value for the mode. Because of the procedure by which the mode is found, it is sometimes referred to as the *inspectional* average.

The median. The median is that point in a distribution which divides the frequencies of the distribution into two equal parts; one-half of the scores will be above this point, and one-half will lie below the point. The procedure for determining the median will differ somewhat depending on the way in which our scores are arranged. If they are arranged in a simple rank-order distribution, such as is found in Fig. 9.2, we will use one set of procedures. If the same scores are arranged in a grouped frequency distribution, such as Fig. 9.4, we will use a different set of procedures. We shall illustrate both sets of procedures.

The procedure for determining the median when scores are arranged in order of rank is a relatively simple one. If the number of scores is an odd number as it is in Fig. 9.2 ($N = 25$), we choose the middle score as the median.[4] The middle score in this distribution would be the thirteenth score counting from either the top or the bottom. In Fig. 9.2, the median is 30. If the number of scores is an even number, the procedure is slightly different. With an even number of scores, we select the *two* middle scores and take a point halfway between them as the median.

When the scores are arranged in a grouped frequency distribution, the procedure for finding the median is somewhat more complex. This increase in complexity is caused by the fact that we have lost the identity

---

[4]These are the procedures usually recommended for calculating the median from ungrouped data. Technically, they may introduce a certain amount of error where the frequency of the midscore is greater than one. For our purposes, however, we can safely ignore this possibility.

of the individual scores when we place them into a grouped frequency distribution. If we have three scores in the interval 24-26, we no longer know whether we had one score each of 24, 25, and 26; whether we had two scores of 24 and one of 26; or whether we had some other of the many possible combinations. Since this knowledge is no longer available to us, we make an assumption about the manner in which the scores are distributed. We assume that the scores in any interval are spread evenly over that interval. Now it is reasonably easy to conceive of this notion when there are three scores to be spread evenly over an interval three score units in length. We can simply visualize this situation as one score per score unit. When we have some other frequency, however, visualization becomes more difficult. If we take the five scores in the interval 30-32 in Fig. 9.4, for example, we must visualize 1 2/3 scores (i.e., 5/3) per unit of measurement.

The procedure for calculating the median from a grouped frequency distribution is illustrated in Fig. 9.8. Note that we have added another column labeled "*cf.*" This is an abbreviation for "cumulative frequency." This expression refers to the process of cumulating (adding in sequential fashion) all values in the frequency column starting with the lowest interval and proceeding upward to the top interval. In Fig. 9.8, for example, the cumulative frequency for the interval 18-20 is 4. This number is the sum of the one frequency in the interval 15-17 and the frequency of three in the interval 18-20. As we proceed up the distribution, we simply add the frequency in each interval to the cumulative frequency of the interval just below it to obtain the cumulative frequency for that particular interval. Thus, the 20 in the *cf* column for the interval 33-35 is the sum of 17 and 3.

We cumulate our frequencies in order to find the middle of our distribution. In this particular distribution, we have 25 scores. The median is defined as the point which separates the frequencies in the distribution into two equal halves, so in this distribution 12.5 scores must lie above the median and 12.5 below the median. The first thing

Figure 9.8 Calculation of the median from a grouped frequency distribution.

Interval	f	cf
45–47	1	25
42–44	1	24
39–41	1	23
36–38	2	22
33–35	3	20
30–32	5	17
27–29	4	12
24–26	3	8
21–23	1	5
18–20	3	4
15–17	1	1
	N = 25	

$$\frac{N}{2} = \frac{25}{2} = 12.5$$

$$12.5 - 12 = 0.5$$

$$\frac{0.5}{5} \times 3 = \frac{1.5}{5} = 0.30$$

$$0.30 + 29.5 = 29.8$$

Median = 29.8

we must do is identify the interval in which the median will be located. We know that the median is identified by the score counting 12.5 from the bottom. We look at our cumulative frequency column and we see a *cf* value of 12 for the interval 27-29. What does this 12 mean? It means that 12 scores have been accumulated starting from the bottom of our distribution, i.e., 14.5, up to the top of that interval, i.e., 29.5. Since we are looking for the point coincident with a cumulative frequency of 12.5, we now know that it must be located somewhere in the interval 30-32. Our next task is to find exactly where in that interval the median will be found.

In locating the median within the mid-interval, we use the assumption mentioned previously, that is, that all of the scores in the interval are spread evenly across the interval. If that is the case, then the 12.5 score lies one-half (12.5–12) of one frequency into the interval. The interval contains five frequencies so the median is located at a point 1/2 /5 or 1/10 of the distance from the bottom of the interval. We need to translate this proportion into our scale of measurement. Each interval is three score units in length so the median is located 1/10 × 3 or 0.3 of a score unit from the bottom of the interval. The bottom of the interval has a real value of 29.5, so we add the additional 0.3 of a unit to it to obtain a value of 29.8 for our median.

Note that the median calculated from the grouped frequency distribution corresponds fairly closely with the median calculated from the same data when they were ungrouped. This demonstrates the relatively small amount of error introduced by grouping procedures.

The mean. The mean[5] is the weighted average of the scores in a distribution; that is, it is the sum of all the score values divided by the number of scores. It is the familiar *average* which you have been calculating since you were in elementary school. Since you now know that there are other averages, you realize the necessity for giving it a special name.

The statistician symbolizes the process of calculating the mean from ungrouped data by the formula

$$M = \frac{\Sigma X}{N},$$

(9.1)

where M is the symbol for the mean,[6] Σ is the capital Greek letter

[5] Technically, this is the arithmetic mean. Since the other means known to the statistician are so very seldom used in educational measurement, they will not be discussed here. Thus, we shall simply refer to the arithmetic mean as "the mean."

[6] Unfortunately, there is as yet no universally accepted set of symbols used by all statisticians. Sometimes, therefore, you may see the symbol $\overline{X}$ used for the mean. The small bar above the X designates a mean value.

"sigma" and indicates the process of summation, X is any score value in the set of scores, and N is the total number of scores in the set.

If we apply this process to our data in their ungrouped form as we find them in Fig. 9.2, we obtain the following result:

$$M = \frac{745}{25} = 29.8$$

When the same data are arranged in a grouped frequency distribution, the procedure for calculating the mean is somewhat different. Again, when our data are in this form, the identity of the individual score has been lost. We must make an assumption as to the location of the scores within each interval. When calculating the mean, we make a different assumption about these scores than the assumption we used when we calculated the median. This time we shall assume that all of the scores in each interval are located at the midpoint of that interval. This assumption is both logically defensible and useful as we shall see.

Figure 9.9 illustrates the method of calculating the mean from a grouped frequency distribution. Immediately to the right of the two columns for interval and frequency, which constitute our basic grouped frequency distribution, we have added a third column labeled X'. The values entered in this column correspond to the midpoints of each of the intervals. They are designated as X' in order to show that the midpoint is being used as a surrogate for the raw score values (the X's) in the interval. This is because we have assumed that all score values in that interval are concentrated at the midpoint of the interval. We can now see why it is important to have a whole number as the midpoint of the interval. Next, we have to take account of the frequencies of each of these midpoints, so we multiply the X' by its corresponding f in order to obtain the fourth column fX'. We sum this column and divide by N to obtain the mean.

Note that this process is logically analogous to the process employed

Figure 9.9 Calculation of the mean from a group frequency distribution.

Interval	f	X'	fX'
45–47	1	46	46
42–44	1	43	43
39–41	1	40	40
36–38	2	37	74
33–35	3	34	102
30–32	5	31	155
27–29	4	28	112
24–26	3	25	75
21–23	1	22	22
18–20	3	19	57
15–17	1	16	16
			742

$$M = \frac{\Sigma fX'}{N} = \frac{742}{25} = 29.68$$

in finding the mean from ungrouped data. There we simply summed the X's. Here we have made two changes. We have substituted X' for X and we have had to take account of the varying frequencies for each X'. In ungrouped data, the frequency for each X is always understood to be one, so frequencies are ignored.

Note also that the mean calculated from the group frequency distribution is not exactly the same as that calculated from the ungrouped data. The amount of error, however, is relatively small.

There is another method of calculating the mean from a grouped frequency distribution which is sometimes referred to as the *short method* because it circumvents a certain amount of calculation. The short method utilizes another statistical concept—the *deviation score*. A deviation score is defined as the deviation (or difference) of a raw score from its mean. The notion of deviation scores is a very valuable one because it can be applied in many different situations.[7]

For purposes of understanding the short method, let us first illustrate it as it might be applied to ungrouped data. Normally, we would never actually use it with ungrouped data because it would effect no saving in time, but the rationale for it can be seen more readily with ungrouped data.

Figure 9.10 provides an example of the calculation of the mean from ungrouped data using the short method. In using this method, our first step is to select an *arbitrary reference point* from which we shall calculate our deviation scores. We shall symbolize this point with the capital letter A and use it instead of the mean as the point from which we are to compute our deviation scores. As we shall see, the reason for this procedure is to reduce the labor involved in our computations. This arbitrary reference point may be any whole number which appears to be approximately in the middle of the distribution. Starting from this point, we are going to calculate the deviation scores corresponding to each raw score value. We shall sum such deviation scores and use them to calculate a *correction factor* to be applied to the arbitrary reference point. The correction factor c is defined as

$$c = \frac{\Sigma d}{N} .$$

Note that in the example provided in Fig. 9.10, we begin by taking an arbitrary reference point at 30 simply because this seemed a convenient place to start. Then we subtracted this value in turn from each of our raw scores and placed the result under the heading d $(d = X - A)$. If the raw score was larger than 30, the result was a positive number. If the raw score was smaller than 30, the result was a negative number.

---

[7] A problem in symbolism arises with the use of deviation scores. The lower case x is normally used to represent such deviation scores, i.e., $x = X - M$. Where deviation scores are calculated, not from the mean but from some arbitrarily selected reference point in the distribution, the symbol d is frequently employed instead. Since we shall be using the latter approach, we shall use d as a symbol for this type of deviation score.

Figure 9.10 Calculating the mean from ungrouped data using the short method.

X	d		
45	+15		
42	+12		
40	+10		
38	+ 8		
37	+ 7		
35	+ 5		
35	+ 5		
33	+ 3		
32	+ 2	$M = A + c$	
31	+ 1		
31	+ 1	$A = 30$	
30	0	$c = \dfrac{\Sigma d}{N} = \dfrac{-5}{25} = -0.2$	
30	0		
29	− 1	$M = 30 + (-0.2) = 29.8$	
29	− 1		
29	− 1		
28	− 2		
26	− 4		
26	− 4		
24	− 6		
23	− 7		
20	−10		
19	−11		
18	−12		
15	−15		
	− 5		

We summed the positive and negative numbers and obtained a sum for the column of -5 ($\Sigma d = -5$). We used this sum to calculate the correction factor which came out to be -0.2 ($C = \Sigma d/N = -5/25 = -0.2$). We added the correction factor to the arbitrary reference point in order to obtain the actual mean of the distribution ($M = A + c = 30 + (-0.2) = 29.8$). Note that, very happily, this value for the mean is the same one we calculated earlier using the regular method. If nothing else, this should provide some assurance that the procedure is a valid one.

Now we should like to take the same idea and apply it to a grouped frequency distribution. To do so, we shall again have to make some minor modifications. These modifications must be made because we lost the identity of the individual scores when we grouped them and because we have varying frequencies for each interval within our grouped distribution. As before, we shall assume that all of our scores are concentrated at the midpoint of each interval so we can use that midpoint (X') to represent each score (X) in the interval. We shall correspondingly define our deviation scores as $d = X' - A$. The reference point will be defined as the midpoint of some interval in the middle of the distribution.

At this point, we introduce an important difference between the procedure for ungrouped data and the one we wish to employ for grouped data. If we look at the magnitude of the d's produced by our procedure, we shall see that each is a multiple of the size of the interval. This occurs, obviously, because we are subtracting the A which itself is the midpoint of an interval from other values which are also midpoints of intervals. Each midpoint is separated from the next by a number equal to the size of the interval. We can take advantage of this fact in our calculations by dividing the deviation scores by the size of the interval used as a constant. Dividing by a constant will not change the relative value of the deviations. Later, we can reintroduce the constant when it comes time to make the correction to our arbitrary reference point.

Figure 9.11 illustrates our procedures. We have chosen 31 as an arbitrary reference point. We have subtracted each midpoint from this point to obtain d and have divided by i, which is the symbol we use for the size of the interval, to obtain the column d/i. We have multiplied each of the values in this column by its appropriate frequency. The sum of the column $f(d/i)$ is -11. We have used this sum to obtain

Figure 9.11 Calculating the mean from a group frequency distribution using the short method.

Interval	f	X'	$\dfrac{d}{i}$	$f\dfrac{d}{i}$
45–47	1	46	+5	+5
42–44	1	43	+4	+4
39–41	1	40	+3	+3
36–38	2	37	+2	+4
33–35	3	34	+1	+3
30–32	5	31	0	0
27–29	4	28	−1	−4
24–26	3	25	−2	−6
21–23	1	22	−3	−3
18–20	3	19	−4	−12
15–17	1	16	−5	−5
				−11

$$M = A + ci \qquad c = \frac{\Sigma f \dfrac{d}{i}}{N} = \frac{-11}{25} = -0.44$$

$$A = 31 \qquad\qquad i = 3$$

$$M = 31 + (-0.44)\,3 = 31 + (-1.32) = 29.68$$

our correction factor, defined as

$$c = \frac{\Sigma f \dfrac{d}{i}}{N}.$$

Since we previously divided each value used in obtaining this correction factor by an amount equal to the size of the interval, we must now reintroduce that constant. Consequently, we multiply the correction factor by the constant i, the size of the interval. As we can see, the magnitude of the mean calculated using the short method agrees with the magnitude obtained by the regular or long method.

Figure 9.12   Two distributions with equal means but different variabilities.

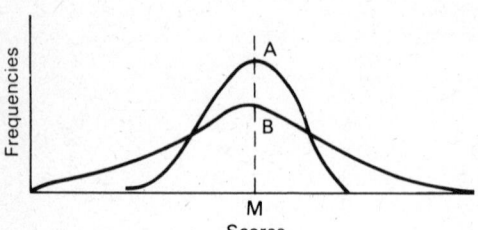

MEASURES OF VARIABILITY

Another basic element in any statistical description of a set of test scores is some measure of variability. We need a measure of variability because knowledge of central tendency alone is not sufficient to give us an accurate description of a set of scores. It is possible for two sets of scores to have the same mean or median and yet be markedly different in variability. Figure 9.12 shows two hypothetical distributions on the same score scale. Note that the means of the two distributions are equal, but that the shapes of the distribution are not the same. The scores of distribution *A* are much more tightly concentrated around the mean, while the scores in distribution *B* are considerably more spread out. Because of the differences which exist among distributions in the spread of scores, we need measures of variability to express this spread. A number of such measures are used by statisticians, but we shall confine our discussion to just three: (1) the *range*, (2) the *quartile deviation*, and (3) the *standard deviation*.

The range. We are already familiar with the range. It is simply the difference between the highest score and the lowest score in a distribution. It can be considered a relatively crude measure of variability because, ordinarily, distributions whose ranges are equal appear to be about equally variable.

The biggest weakness of the range is that its value is determined by

Figure 9.13 Two distributions with equal ranges.

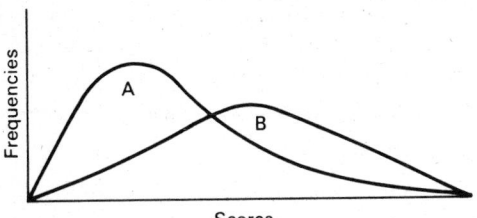

the two extreme scores in a distribution. Where distributions are shaped somewhat symmetrically, this is no real problem. Where a distribution is markedly skewed, however, the range can give a misleading picture of variability. Consider the two distributions in Fig. 9.13, for example. Both distributions have the same range, yet it is obvious that the scores in both distributions are really not equally variable. The scores in distribution A are much more tightly concentrated than those in distribution B. It is only because of the long tail of distribution A that its range is equal to that of distribution B.

The semi-interquartile range. The semi-interquartile range (also called the quartile deviation) is a somewhat more stable measure of variability than the range. It is defined as half the range between the first and third quartiles. The formula for the semi-interquartile range is given as follows:

$$Q = \frac{Q_3 - Q_1}{2} , \tag{9.2}$$

where Q is the semi-interquartile range, Q_3 is the third quartile, and Q_1 is the first quartile.

The quartiles are those points in a distribution which divide the distribution into fourths. That is, 25 percent of the scores will lie above Q_3; 25 percent will lie below Q_1; and 25 percent will lie each between Q_1 to Q_2 to Q_3.

The quartile deviation can be described as the *average* interquartile range. Why the average? Why not simply take the range between Q_1 and Q_2 or Q_2 and Q_3? The answer is that these two distances will not always be equal. They will be equal only when the distribution is perfectly symmetrical. If the distribution is not symmetrical, they will always differ to some extent. Since a perfectly symmetrical distribution is an extremely rare occurrence in real life, the average interquartile range provides a better estimate of variability than either of the individual interquartile ranges taken by itself.

The standard deviation. Both the range and the quartile deviation have one basic weakness as measures of variability. Both are determined by only two points in a distribution. The quartile deviation tends to be somewhat more stable than the range because the two points which determine it are located further inside the distribution, where less fluctuation is likely to occur. In either case, however, the information about variability provided by all of the scores in the distribution is not used. If such information were to be used, a much more stable measure of variability would result. The most commonly used measure of variability which meets this specification is the standard deviation.

The standard deviation is defined as the square root of the mean of the squared deviation scores of a distribution. Symbolically, the definition looks like this:

$$\sigma = \sqrt{\frac{\Sigma x^2}{N}}, \tag{9.3}$$

where σ is the lower-case Greek letter "sigma" which is used to designate the standard deviation, x is a deviation score $(X - M)$, and N is the number of scores in the set of scores.

This definitional formula for the standard deviation is relatively simple, but it is difficult to use in actual computations. Deviation scores are readily computed where the mean is a whole number, but this is very seldom the case. Where the mean is a mixed number such as the 29.8 we calculated for our ungrouped data earlier in this chapter, computing and squaring deviation scores can become something of a chore. The process is also likely to produce simple arithmetic errors. Because of this we usually employ *computational* formulas in place of the definitional formula for the standard deviation. These computational formulas are based on the same logic used in calculating the mean by the short method.

Let us illustrate the computation of the standard deviation from ungrouped data using two of these computational formulas. The two formulas are given in this fashion:

$$\sigma = \sqrt{\left[\frac{\Sigma d^2}{N} - c^2\right]}, \qquad (9.4)$$

where d^2 is the square of a deviation score calculated from an arbitrary reference point and c^2 is the square of the correction factor and is equal to $(\Sigma d/N)^2$.

The second formula we shall use is algebraically equivalent to the first and can be demonstrated to be equivalent to the first formula if an arbitrary reference point is taken at zero. The formula is:

$$\sigma = \sqrt{\left[\frac{\Sigma X^2}{N} - M^2\right]}, \qquad (9.5)$$

where X^2 is the square of a raw score, M^2 is the mean squared, and N is the number of scores.

Figure 9.14 shows the computation of the standard deviation using both formulas. Note that the answer comes out the same regardless of the formula employed. The raw-score formula (9.5) is somewhat more cumbersome for paper-and-pencil computation. However, if a desk calculator (or a computer) is available the second formula is preferred.

Figure 9.14 Calculation of the standard deviation from ungrouped data.

	Formula 1			Formula 2
X	d	d^2	X	X^2
45	+15	225	45	2025
42	+12	144	42	1764
40	+10	100	40	1600
38	+ 8	64	38	1444
37	+ 7	49	37	1369
35	+ 5	25	35	1225
35	+ 5	25	35	1225
33	+ 3	9	33	1089
32	+ 2	4	32	1024
31	+ 1	1	31	961
31	+ 1	1	31	961
30	0	0	30	900
30	0	0	30	900
29	− 1	1	29	841
29	− 1	1	29	841
29	− 1	1	29	841
28	− 2	4	28	784
26	− 4	16	26	676
26	− 4	16	26	676
24	− 6	36	24	576
23	− 7	49	23	529
20	−10	100	20	400
19	−11	121	19	361
18	−12	144	18	324
15	−15	225	15	225
	− 5	1361	745	23561

$$\sqrt{\frac{1361}{25} - \left(\frac{-5}{25}\right)^2} = \sqrt{54.44 - 0.04}$$

$$\sqrt{54.40} = 7.38$$

$$\sqrt{\frac{23561}{25} - \frac{745}{25}^2}$$

$$\sqrt{942.44 - 888.04}$$

$$\sqrt{54.40} = 7.38$$

The same procedures can be applied to a grouped frequency distribution with appropriate changes to the formulas. When using the short method, the formula for the standard deviation calculated from a grouped frequency distribution looks like this:

$$\sigma = i \sqrt{\frac{\Sigma f \frac{d^2}{i}}{N} - \left(\frac{\Sigma f \frac{d}{i}}{N}\right)^2} \qquad (9.6)$$

The procedure given in formula (9.6) is illustrated in Fig. 9.15. Note that, as in the case of the mean, we divide the deviations from arbitrary reference point by a constant equal to the size of the interval. We must thus reintroduce this constant by multiplying everything under the radical sign by the size of the interval.

The other formula for calculating the standard deviation from a grouped frequency distribution is given by the following formula:

$$\sigma = \sqrt{\frac{\Sigma f(X')^2}{N} - M^2} . \qquad (9.7)$$

Figure 9.15 Calculating the standard deviation from a grouped frequency distribution using the short method.

Interval	f	$\frac{d}{i}$	$f\frac{d}{i}$	$f\left(\frac{d}{i}\right)^2$
45–47	1	+5	+5	25
42–44	1	+4	+4	16
39–41	1	+3	+3	9
36–38	2	+2	+4	8
33–35	3	+1	+3	3
30–32	5	0	0	0
27–29	4	−1	−4	4
24–26	3	−2	−6	12
21–23	1	−3	−3	9
18–20	3	−4	−12	48
15–17	1	−5	−5	25
			−11	159

$\sigma = 3\sqrt{159/25 - (-11/25)^2} = 3\sqrt{6.36 - 0.19}$

$= 3\sqrt{6.17} = 3 \times 2.484 = 7.45$

This formula uses the midpoints of the intervals to represent the scores and uses the mean squared as a correction factor. Note that the quantity under the radical sign is *not* multiplied by i in this formula because the deviations, which in this case are the differences between the arbitrary reference point and the midpoints of the intervals, have not been divided by i as a constant. This formula is identical to formula (9.5) used in finding the standard deviation from ungrouped data with the exception that X' has been substituted for X and f has been added to take account of the varying frequencies. The computation of the standard deviation from a grouped frequency distribution using this formula is illustrated in Fig. 9.16.

Frequently after having calculated a standard deviation, students will ask what it is. The intricacies of calculation, as they perceive them, have tended to obfuscate the meaning of the end product. The standard deviation is, of course, a measure of the relative variability of test scores around their mean. Distributions with large standard deviations

Figure 9.16 Calculating the standard deviation from a grouped frequency distribution using the midpoints of intervals.

Interval	f	X'	fX'	$f(X')^2$
45–47	1	46	46	2116
42–44	1	43	43	1849
39–41	1	40	40	1600
36–38	2	37	74	2738
33–35	3	34	102	3468
30–32	5	31	155	4805
27–29	4	28	112	3136
24–26	3	25	75	1875
21–23	1	22	22	484
18–20	3	19	57	1083
15–17	1	16	16	256
			742	23410

$$\sigma = \sqrt{23410/25 - (742/25)^2} = \sqrt{936.4 - 880.9}$$
$$= \sqrt{55.5} = 7.45$$

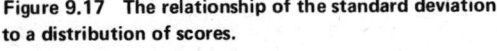

Figure 9.17 The relationship of the standard deviation to a distribution of scores.

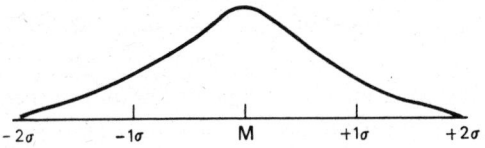

have scores which are more variable than the scores of distributions with smaller standard deviations.

It is well to remember that the standard deviation is a linear distance along the X axis (abscissa) of a distribution measured above and below the mean. Figure 9.17 illustrates this point. The number of standard deviations in a distribution is to a considerable extent a function of the number of scores. Note that in our distribution of 25 scores which has a range of 30 points (45-15), there are approximately four standard deviations, i.e., $4 \times 7.45 = 29.80$, or nearly 30. Where the distribution has a much larger number of scores, you would expect to find a larger number of standard deviations comprising the range. Seldom, however, would you find more than six standard deviations in your range. This bit of knowledge provides a convenient way for checking the accuracy of your computations of the standard deviation. Simply determine the range, divide it by 4, and see if your calculated figure is anywhere in the near vicinity. If it is not, you have probably made a mistake.

SCORE TRANSFORMATIONS

Up to this point in our discussion of the statistical treatment of test scores, we have been concerned with those procedures which help us attribute meaning to a test score by allowing us to make comparisons between that score and other scores in the same distribution. There are occasions, however, when we wish to make comparisons between distributions. If we use raw scores, we find ourselves severely handicapped in making such comparisons. Suppose, for example, we are told that Johnny received a score of 42 on a spelling test and a score of 37 on an arithmetic test. On which test did he demonstrate higher achievement? We realize that the raw scores themselves tell us very little. What we need is some measure which will give us Johnny's relative position on both tests. Then we can make a comparison from one test to the other. The major purpose of score transformations is to allow us to make such direct comparisons. We shall discuss the two major types of such transformations: (1) *standard scores,* and (2) *percentile ranks.*

Standard scores. Standard scores are so called because they are based on the standard deviation. Any standard-score system will enable you to tell where a given score is located in its distribution. Essentially the standard score tells you how many standard deviations above or below the mean this score is located.

Most standard-score systems are based on z, the *standard measure.* A z score is defined as

$$z = \frac{X - M}{\sigma}, \qquad (9.8)$$

where z is the standard measurement equivalent of a raw score, X is any given raw score, M is the mean of the distribution of raw scores, of which X is a member, and σ is the standard deviation of that distribution.

Once raw scores are converted to z scores, all such sets of scores have identical means and standard deviations. The mean of a set of z scores is always 0, and the standard deviation is always equal to 1. A raw score which in its original distribution was located one and one-half standard deviations below the mean would have a z score equivalent of -1.5. Similarly, one located two-thirds of a standard deviation above the mean would have a z score equivalent of $+0.67$. Thus a score always tells you how many standard deviations above or below the mean that particular score was located.

The major advantage of z scores over raw scores is that z scores from different distributions can be directly compared. In Johnny's case, if we knew that his raw score of 42 in spelling was equivalent to a z score of +1.12 and his raw score of 37 on arithmetic was equal to +1.39, we know immediately that he scored higher in arithmetic than in spelling. Naturally, we have to exercise some caution in interpreting z scores where the z scores for the tests we are comparing differ greatly in the size of the groups tested, but where we are making comparisons within our own classroom, this is not a problem.

One disadvantage of z scores, at least in the opinion of many people, is that half the scores have negative values. Many persons dislike working with negative numbers. In addition, there are some who feel a kind of stigma attached to negative numbers especially when they are associated with test scores. For this reason, a number of different types of standard scores have been evolved which provide systems of scores all of which have positive numbers. All that is necessary to devise such a system is to decide upon a number you would like for a mean, decide upon a number for a standard deviation, and substitute them into the general formula

$$S = M + sz, \tag{9.9}$$

where S is a symbol for the standard score, M is the value for the mean, s is the value for the standard deviation, and z is the standard measure.

Figure 9.18 shows a number of such standard scores. Note that T scores have a mean of 50 and a standard deviation of 10, CEEB (College Entrance Examination Board) scores have a mean of 500 and a standard deviation of 100; AGCT (Army General Classification Test) scores have a mean of 100 and a standard deviation of 20. Also notice the IQ's on the Wechsler Scales given at the bottom of Fig. 9.18. The Wechsler

Figure 9.18   Relationships among various types of derived scores.[a]

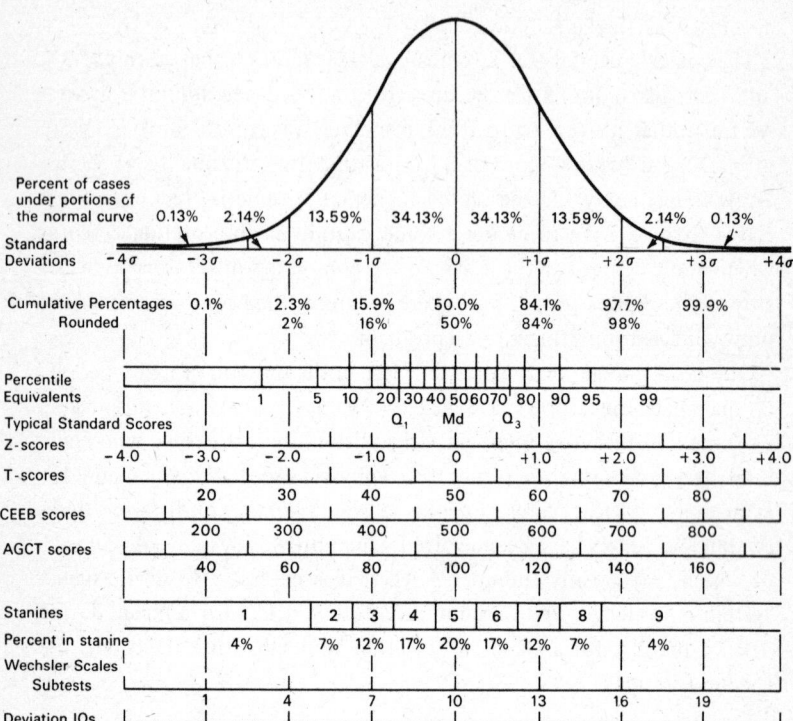

[a]From H. G. Seashore, ed., "Methods of Expressing Test Scores," *Test Service Bulletin*, No. 48, 1955 (The Psychological Corporation, New York).

Scales are individual intelligence tests. The IQ's on these scales exemplify a trend which is now nearly universal; that is, the IQ's are now standard scores (also called deviation IQ's) rather than the familiar ratio ($IQ = MA/CA \times 100$) which was used for so many years.

In addition to providing a ready method of comparison, standard scores serve another function. They allow us to combine scores from different tests to give equal weight (or predetermined differential weight) to the tests. It is a common practice of teachers to add the raw scores from two or more tests to obtain a composite distribution. They then use this composite distribution as a basis for assigning grades for the term. The practice is perfectly defensible so long as the teacher is aware of what is occurring. When raw scores from different tests are added together, each such score is given a *natural* weighting equal to the variability of its distribution. Many times, however, teachers claim that they wish to give equal weight to the results of two tests. So long as the variability of the tests is nearly the same, simply adding the scores together will do this. If the variabilities are different, however, one set of test scores will invariably receive greater weight than the other. A teacher can avoid this difficulty by converting raw scores to standard scores. Since standard scores by definition have equal variability, they can always be added directly together to give equal weight. Standard scores can also be used to give differential weight to tests. The teacher may wish, for example, to weight one test twice as heavily as another. When using standard scores, all that is necessary in order to do this is to double the magnitude of the standard scores from that test before adding it to the standard score from the other test.

Special mention should be made of that type of standard score known as a *stanine*. "Stanine" is a portmanteau expression combining portions of the two words "standard" and "nine." It refers to the process of dividing a distribution into nine parts (seven of which are equal in linear distance along the baseline) using the standard deviation as a means for making the divisions. Figure 9.18 also shows the divisions for the nine stanine values based on a normal distribution.

Converting raw scores to stanines can be very useful to the teacher who wishes to combine the results of a number of tests. To do this we normally employ a table such as that given in Table 9.1. To use such a table, we simply arrange our raw scores in order of magnitude and then assign stanine equivalents to raw scores beginning at either the top or bottom of our scale. If, for example, we had 30 students in our class, the top ranking score would receive a stanine value of 9; the next two

TABLE 9.1 TABLE OF STANINES.

Size of Group	Stanines								
	1	2	3	4	5	6	7	8	9
	Number of Individuals Receiving Stanine Score								
20	1	1	2	4	4	4	2	1	1
21	1	1	2	4	5	4	2	1	1
22	1	2	2	4	4	4	2	2	1
23	1	2	2	4	5	4	2	2	1
24	1	2	3	4	4	4	3	2	1
25	1	2	3	4	5	4	3	2	1
26	1	2	3	4	6	4	3	2	1
27	1	2	3	5	5	5	3	2	1
28	1	2	3	5	6	5	3	2	1
29	1	2	4	5	5	5	4	2	1
30	1	2	4	5	6	5	4	2	1
31	1	2	4	5	7	5	4	2	1
32	1	2	4	6	6	6	4	2	1
33	1	2	4	6	7	6	4	2	1
34	1	3	4	6	6	6	4	3	1
35	1	3	4	6	7	6	4	3	1
36	1	3	4	6	8	6	4	3	1
37	2	3	4	6	7	6	4	3	2
38	1	3	5	6	8	6	5	3	1
39	1	3	5	7	7	7	5	3	1
40	1	3	5	7	8	7	5	3	1
41	1	3	5	7	9	7	5	3	1
42	2	3	5	7	8	7	5	3	2
43	2	3	5	7	9	7	5	3	2
44	2	3	5	8	8	8	5	3	2
45	2	3	5	8	9	8	5	3	2
46	2	3	5	8	10	8	5	3	2
47	2	3	6	8	9	8	6	3	2
48	2	3	6	8	10	8	6	3	2
49	2	4	6	8	9	8	6	4	2
50	2	3	6	9	10	9	6	3	2
51	2	3	6	9	11	9	6	3	2
52	2	4	6	9	10	9	6	4	2
53	2	4	6	9	11	9	6	4	2
54	2	4	7	9	10	9	7	4	2
55	2	4	7	9	11	9	7	4	2
56	2	4	7	9	12	9	7	4	2

TABLE 9.1 (cont'd.)

Size of Group	Stanines								
	1	2	3	4	5	6	7	8	9
	Number of Individuals Receiving Stanine Score								
57	2	4	7	10	11	10	7	4	2
58	2	4	7	10	12	10	7	4	2
59	3	4	7	10	11	10	7	4	3
60	3	4	7	10	12	10	7	4	3

scores would receive stanines of 8; the next four would receive a 7; and so on down to the bottom score which would receive a stanine of 1. Stanines may be treated as any other standard score, adding them together to give equal weight to tests, or multiplying them by some number to give differential weight.

Some teachers object to the use of stanines because they feel they are "losing information" when they convert raw scores to stanines. The raw score looks more precise because it is usually a larger number and comes from a distribution having more variability. It is true that a certain amount of differential information is indeed lost when using stanines. Unless the original measures are highly reliable, however, the loss is not likely to be great. The greater versatility and ease of handling of stanines more than compensate for the small loss of differential information.

Percentile ranks. The percentile rank is a type of score transformation that is even more widely used than standard scores. Likely this occurs because it is somewhat easier to understand and to calculate. The percentile rank of a score is defined as the percentage of scores lying below the given score point, in other words, below the midpoint of the interval represented by that score. If, for example, we say that a given score has a percentile rank (symbolized as PR) of 77, we mean that 77 percent of the scores in the distribution lie below the score point. Conversely, 23 percent would lie above this point.

Percentile ranks provide a convenient way to make comparisons between scores. If we know that Johnny's test score in spelling had a percentile rank of 87 while his score in arithmetic had a percentile rank of 92, we know immediately that he stood somewhat higher in arithmetic than in spelling. Moreover, we know exactly what the two numbers 87 and 92 mean. Undoubtedly, this simplicity of meaning of percentile ranks contributes to their wide acceptance.

The method of calculating percentile ranks from ungrouped data is illustrated in Fig. 9.19. The procedure is fairly simple. You begin by setting up a "Score" column which begins one point higher than your largest observed score and goes one point lower than your lowest observed score. Then you set up a "Double tallies" column. Each raw score in your set of scores is to be tallied twice. The purpose of the double tally is to take into account the fact that each score is an interval rather than a point. By tallying each score twice, once at a

Figure 9.19 Calculation of percentile ranks for ungrouped data.

Score	Double Tallies	cf	PR	Score	Double Tallies	cf	PR
46		50	100	29	///	21	42
45	/	49	98	28	/	17	34
44		48	96	27		16	32
43		48	96	26	//	14	28
42	/	47	94	25		12	24
41		46	92	24	/	11	22
40	/	45	90	23	/	9	18
39		44	88	22		8	16
38	/	43	86	21		8	16
37	/	41	82	20	/	7	14
36		40	80	19	/	5	10
35	//	38	76	18	/	3	6
34		36	72	17		2	4
33	/	35	70	16		2	4
32	/	33	66	15	/	1	2
31	//	30	60	14		0	0
30	//	26	52				

position below the midpoint of the score and once at a position above the midpoint of the score, we can take into account the continuous nature of the variation with which we are dealing. Next we cumulate these tallies beginning at the bottom and working to the top. The cumulative frequency for each score represents the cumulated tallies up to that score point or midpoint for that score. The last step is simply to turn each *cf* into a *PR* (percentile rank) through the use of the formula

$$PR = \frac{cf}{2N} \times 100. \qquad (9.10)$$

In our set of scores, $N = 25$. Thus the percentile rank for a raw score of 38 is equal to

$$PR = \frac{43}{2(25)} \times 100 = \frac{43}{50} \times 100 = 86.$$

Once the conversion for raw scores to percentile ranks has been made, the percentile rank for any score in the set can be read directly from the table.

Notice that in theory, no observed score in a distribution can have a percentile rank of 100 or 0. The reason for this is that percentile ranks are always calculated from the score point or midpoint of a score, and theoretically, half the score lies above this point and half the score lies below the point. Thus, even for the highest score in a set of scores, half of that score lies above the score point from which its percentile rank is calculated. Similarly, for the lowest score in a set of scores, half of that score lies below the score point. In actual practice, where the number of scores is very large, as in standardized tests for example, percentile ranks of 100 and 0 are sometimes reported simply because we normally round to the nearest whole number.

A final word. We have suggested in this chapter that the relative position of a score within a group of scores should be used as the basis for assigning meaning to that score. Standard scores and percentile ranks are statistical transformations designed to facilitate this process.

The teacher's concern is to judge the quality of the performance indicated by the score. He will be interested in making judgments of good or poor, satisfactory or unsatisfactory. We do not suggest that the relative position of the student's score within his group should be the only criterion considered in making these judgments. Certainly the general level of proficiency of the group itself needs to be taken into account. A low score in a superior group is not the same as a low score in a less able group. Also, it may be desirable to consider the aptitude of the student in assessing the quality of his performance. The level of proficiency required for the slow learning child might reasonably be lower than that for the more able child. It might be well to note that the designation "slow-learning" child is a relative one and implies comparison to other children.

There are, then, such additional factors to be considered. No standard answers can be given to the problems raised. The answers depend on the values held by the individual teacher and upon the policies of the particular school district. Whatever the value system used, it has been our contention that any judgments should be based on the most valid criteria the teacher can employ. The principal purpose of this book has been to improve the validity of those criteria.

10
GRADING
AND
REPORTING

One of the chief aims of this book has been to help the classroom teacher devise more valid instruments for assessing educational achievement. The chief justification for such an aim is an educational one. Through an improvement of tests and testing procedures, the teacher can more effectively know the attainments of his students and judge how well they have met his expectations of them as set in his statements of objectives. Having defined what he means by *achievement* with his statements of objectives, the teacher can then produce valid evidence to demonstrate whether or not these objectives have been met. If they have not, steps can be taken to ensure that the objectives will be met in the future or else to call into question the appropriateness of the objectives for this course and this level of study.

On the other hand, any teacher knows that not all of the activities in which he engages are completely justified on the basis of educational benefit to the student. One such activity is grading. Teachers have long accepted grading as a type of necessary evil. Given free choice in the matter, most teachers would probably reject grading as an integral part of the teaching process. They would feel that claims made for the necessity of grading, claims based on such notions as motivation, feedback, guidance, and so forth, are no more than mere rationalizations, and that education could proceed equally as well in the absence of any type of grading.

Teachers, however, do not have the ultimate say in education. Education is a social institution, and those members of society who see the need for and who support education are also interested in knowing the outcomes of the process. They are seldom completely satisfied by terminal rites such as promotions and graduations. Particularly in the case of their own children, people wish to know the progress students are making. Many would like a daily accounting if it could be made available to them. Since practicality precludes such a procedure, they will settle for something less, but in no case will they do without reports entirely. Thus the pressure for reporting educational progress comes not from teachers but from those who pay the bill for education and who demand to see the results of their expenditures.

Teachers should not be too quick to condemn a society that demands evidence of educational achievement. At no time in previous history has any society been so dependent upon the school for its continued existence. We know that if our schools fail, we also fail. A technological society cannot exist in the absence of a broad, educational base. Parents may not be able to verbalize this observation is syllogistic fashion, but they are aware, if only dimly, that students must succeed in school if our way of life is to be maintained. So they demand evidence that students are succeeding. They may not be overly critical or sophisticated in the type of evidence they require, but they do demand some type of evidence. School marks and grades answer this demand.

Teachers are as well aware as anyone of the deficiencies of grades and marks as evidence of school achievement. Although they might not use the term, they recognize that grades are not perfectly valid. They recognize that this invalidity includes weaknesses in both reliability and relevance. Chance plays a large part in the grade a student receives, chance in the particular teacher to whom he is assigned, chance in the many variables affecting the teacher, the group, and the instructional situation. All such factors affect the reliability of grades. Teachers are also frequently unsure of their objectives, and in the absence of such cannot be certain that the grades they assign represent real differences among students. Moreover, they may have allowed extraneous factors such as conduct, effort, or personality to influence their judgments. To the extent such factors obtain, grades are less relevant than they could be.

Although we recognize that grades are not perfectly valid, we should not conclude that they are completely invalid and useless. They do serve several useful functions.

1. Grades provide a means of reporting student achievement to parents. This is undoubtedly their chief function and has already been considered.

2. Grades provide feedback to students regarding their achievement. The feedback function has probably been overrated, especially the claims made for facilitating learning. As a form of reinforcement, grades are much too infrequent and much too removed temporally from the act of learning to have a significant effect on the learning process.

3. Grades motivate students to learn. Students, particularly older ones, will work for grades. Many critics deprecate the use of grades for this purpose because they claim that grades represent an *external* incentive, and students should rather be motivated by an internal incentive, i.e., the love of learning. While internal incentives may be preferable, external ones do affect human behavior. The most vocal critics of grades on this account probably themselves work for salaries.

4. Grades provide useful information for guiding students in their

vocational and educational plans. Since grades do provide an index of success in academic activities, they can be used by the student to help make choices about future plans. There is little point in planning a professional career for the student whose grades reflect an inability to master verbal or mathematical materials.

5. Grades give a basis for predicting future academic success. Our best single indication of how well a student will perform academically in future years is how well he has performed in the past. Recognizing this fact the usual admission procedure to most colleges places heavy emphasis upon student grades.

6. Grades are convenient in keeping permanent school records. Such records are almost always kept for all students who have ever been in attendance at a school. High-school principals are frequently requested to write letters of recommendation for former students, occasionally for students who were graduated a number of years in the past. Grades entered on permanent records provide a convenient indication of the students' relative achievements.

7. Grades can be used in certifying levels of accomplishment. Schools must still make decisions about promotions and graduations. In the absence of more relevant information, school officials can use grades as a major aid to making such decisions.

It should be noted that these functions may not always be compatible. A grading procedure designed to serve one function effectively may be ineffective in serving another. The most informative procedure for reporting achievement to parents may provide little basis for predicting future academic success.

Regardless of any attempts we might make to justify the practice of grading, teachers will continue to regard it as an onerous chore. They will continue to regard it as one of the least rewarding aspects of their job. Perhaps this is because grading inevitably places the teacher in the role of judge and because, regardless of how much we may refine the validity of our grades and regardless of how loudly we may proclaim that a grade should be viewed as a measurement and not as an evaluation of personal worth, students feel that it is still good to be number one. The student who is not number one knows that, on this measure at least, he is not. Teachers do not like to tell students that their achievement is not all it might be. They prefer the role of friendly helper or counselor, taking each student as they find him and assisting him on his way to the maximum benefit that might accrue to him from his educational experience. Somehow assigning grades seems incompatible with this role.

If we must assign grades, and it appears that in many situations we must, our grades should be as valid as we can possibly make them. The validity of our grades is primarily determined by the validity of the instruments we use to assess student achievement. Most of this book has been directed toward the improvement of this type of validity, but validity in grading also depends upon such things as the type of system we employ, the methods we use for translating scores into grades, and the methods we employ for combining several measures into composite scores. All of these things we propose to discuss in this chapter.

REPORTING

Grading and reporting are not the same thing. When a teacher assigns a grade, that grade may serve a number of purposes. One such purpose is to inform the parents or guardians of a child how well that child is doing in school. This process of informing parents of a child's progress is what we mean by *reporting.*

When we think of reporting to parents, we tend automatically to think of report cards. Undoubtedly this is because the report card has been the traditional way of sending information about a child's academic progress home to his parents. But modern schools do not restrict reporting techniques to report cards alone. They employ, in addition, the personal letter and the teacher-parent conference. We should like to discuss all three approaches.

Report cards. There is considerable variation in the amount and type of information contained on a school report card. Historically, the older report cards contained little other than a listing of the subjects the student was studying, the grades he was receiving in these subjects, and some indication of "deportment," or how well he was behaving in school. In the 1930s, however, the format of report cards underwent considerable transformation. Some evaluation of personality characteristics became almost as common as evaluation of academic achievement. Various types of check lists or rating scales were used in place of numerical or alphabetical grading systems. All this was in keeping with the emphasis on development of the "whole child." Nowadays this emphasis has declined somewhat, but report cards still how the signs of their ancestry. Typically they include both information on academic achievement and information of the teacher's assessment of relevant personal characteristics of the student.

It is difficult to defend any one type of report card as intrinsically superior to others. About the most that can be said is that any well designed report card should include the following pieces of information:

1. The name of the child and possibly those of the parents or guardians.

2. The number of days of school attended and the number of days absent.

3. The grades for the term whether these are given as letter grades, numerical grades, or checks on a check list or rating scale.

4. Some space for comments by the teacher.

5. A place for the signature of one of the parents, if the card is to be returned to the school.

Information on such things as effort, leadership, citizenship, and so forth are supplemental in nature. Whether they are to be included on a report card depends upon the philosophy of education held by the teachers, the administration, and the school board. If assessment of personality characteristics is deemed to be the equal of assessment of academic achievement, then, naturally, these items will be included.

Many school districts are now experimenting with preparing reports by computer. This will undoubtedly become more common as computer facilities become more available. The major advantage of computer reporting is the saving in teacher time which will ultimately be realized. At the moment, this saving in time may not be so apparent because the necessary procedures have not been sufficiently refined. The biggest disadvantage of computer-prepared reports is that they do not provide opportunity for any personal comments by the teacher. Many teachers may consider this an advantage rather than a disadvantage because they are then relieved of the necessity of saying something special about each of their numerous students. If something special needs to be said, perhaps the personal letter is a more appropriate medium than the report card.

Personal letters. The major advantage of the personal letter is the fact that it speaks directly and uniquely to the individual child and his parents. The teacher can present in detail his assessment of the progress of the child and also his basis for that assessment. The parents may receive more useful information and be more aware of how the teacher really feels.

The personal letter has two major disadvantages, however. First, it is difficult to write. Many teachers have never developed the knack of writing a letter which conveys an accurate summary of the achievement of the child without unduly annoying the parents. Some schools have experienced so much difficulty with personal letters that they have drawn up outlines for teachers to follow in writing such letters. Naturally, this tends to restrict the scope of the letter somewhat and may lead to an artificial and stilted production. Second, and more obvious, it takes a great deal of time. Even in the elementary school where a teacher may have no more than 30 students, it is difficult to write such letters more than once a year. It takes time to gather the information to go into the letter; it takes time to think of something original or novel to say about each child; it takes time to write the letter. In a secondary school where a teacher may have 150 students, the task becomes prohibitive.

Schools that have tried to use the personal letter as a substitute for the report card have almost universally found it impossible to do so. In addition to the difficulty encountered in their preparation, personal letters rarely contain all of the same information about the achievement of a student that can be conveyed more simply and more accurately in a report card. While the personal letter may serve the reporting function very well, it is less useful and much more cumbersome for maintaining permanent school records. It should, therefore, be considered a supplement to, rather than a substitute for, the report card.

Parent-teacher conferences. In some ways, the parent-teacher conference is superior to the personal letter as a means of conveying information. For one thing, the teacher does not have to spend time writing even though there may be no particular saving of time in gathering information. For another thing, there is less likelihood of misunderstanding between parent and teacher because the personal contact allows the teacher to explain at greater length and to clarify any misconceptions that a parent may have developed. In addition, a conference is likely to lead to better rapport between parent and teacher than a letter would. Because of such advantages as these most schools, particularly elementary schools, make some provision for such conferences.

There are no inflexible rules which can be given governing the conduct of a parent-teacher conference. Certain suggestions, however, might be in order.

1. Allow at least a half hour for each conference. This much time is needed in case the parent wishes to discuss his child's progress at some length.

2. Schedule time for the conference as part of the normal work load. Do not "tack it on" at the end of the regular school day. This is the responsibility of the principal of the school, but the teachers should insist on it.

3. Have information about the child ready at the time of the conference. Some teachers have manila folders with examples of the child's work. Others use summary sheets giving test results, grades, personality assessments, or other relevant data. Whatever form it may take, the information should be readily available and accessible so no time is lost looking for it.

4. Anticipate the type of questions the parent may ask. The ability to do this depends, in large part, upon experience, but even the inexperienced teacher can guess at the kind of things Johnny's mother may wish to know.

5. Be prepared to listen attentively if the parent has gripes or grievances to air. It is natural for us to react defensively if our efforts and intentions are judged less than perfect, but defensive behavior never wins friends or influences parents. If it is apparent that the feelings expressed are sufficiently intense that a half-hour conference cannot ameliorate them, an additional conference should be scheduled in the near future.

Difficulties in scheduling probably represent the biggest weakness in parent-teacher conferences. Some parents have no free time in the afternoon because of their jobs and, hence, can never come to a conference. Other parents will agree to come and never show up. Others may call at the last minute and wish to change the time or date of their appointment. All of these are trials the teacher must bear with equanimity if the proper functions of the parent-teacher conference are to be preserved.

GRADING

We can begin our discussion of grading with two general observations. First, it is reasonably safe to say that there is no perfect system. Any method which is proposed can be shown to possess deficiencies. Second, all systems of grading are ultimately subjective and relative. They are subjective because the grade must be assigned on the basis of the judgment of one or more persons. They are relative in the sense that, regardless of teacher protestation to the contrary, the final basis for a given grade rests on the teacher's experience with other students; that is, the grade is based on a comparison of the achievement of the individual student with that of some group of students.

When grading was introduced, the group to which comparisons were made was, theoretically at least, all students at the particular grade level in school. There was frequently the assumption that the curriculum at each grade level consisted of certain, specified subject matter to be "mastered." The student who did not master this subject matter was retained at that grade level until he had done so or had given up the effort and quit school.

Under these conditions an increasing number of students were doomed to failure as social pressure and compulsory education laws led toward practically universal education. Students of lower ability, who previously would have been eliminated early from the school population, were then required to attend. As a result, schools moved toward a policy of automatic promotion with retention limited to the few students who it was felt would benefit by the repetition of the grade level. At the same time teachers attempted, at least for the slow-learning child, to take the ability of the pupil into account in evaluating his achievement. At present, this policy is almost universally accepted at the elementary level. It is widely accepted at the high-school level although distinctions are frequently made on the basis of the type of curriculum or program. Ability is rarely taken into account at the collegiate level. This variation suggests the possibility, if not the desirability, of using different grading systems at different levels of school.

A number of different grading systems can be found in modern schools. We will consider here only those most frequently encountered.

The percentage system. The percentage system is likely the oldest system of grading still in use. As the name would imply, this system uses a 100-point scale for designating the level of achievement. Operationally, fewer than 100 points are used since extremely low numbers tend to be avoided as grades. Under this system Johnny might receive a grade of 88 in spelling, 91 in arithmetic, and 77 in reading. Until the early part of the twentieth century, almost all schools used this percentage system.

The percentage scale began to lose its popularity as teachers and administrators began to question its basic assumptions. One such assumption dealt with the meaning of the word "percentage." If the grade was a percentage, of what was it a percent? The traditional answer was that it represented the ratio between actual achievement and maximum possible achievement for the student. That is, the student who received a grade of 91 in arithmetic had achieved 91 percent of maximum possible achievement in arithmetic for that grade level. For this reason, the system was frequently called an *absolute* system of grading because the grade represented that proportion of potentially possible knowledge and skill which the individual student had attained. But gradually teachers were forced to acknowledge that the notion of a known and definable measure of maximum achievement was indefensible. No one can really define or measure maximum possible achievement in fourth-grade arithmetic. It became apparent that the denominator of the ratio was not really maximum possible achievement, but rather the individual teacher's conception of this quantity, defined, most likely, by the number and kinds of items on a test. The problem would become even more complicated if one attempted to define the grade as a percent of the maximum achievement that the pupil could attain at his level of ability.

It also became apparent that a 100-point scale was probably too refined to accommodate the known inaccuracies of teacher judgment. Could a teacher really discriminate between a score of 88 and one of 89, or was the one-point difference largely a matter of error? There were many who believed that a scale employing fewer categories would more accurately reflect the type of judgments teachers were capable of making. As a result the percentage system was largely superseded by the five-point scale or *letter* scale of grading as it is more commonly called.

It should be made clear that there is nothing inherently wrong with a system of grading using a scale of 0–100. It is simply a mistake to refer to such a scale as a "percentage" scale because this interpretation is indefensible. So long, however, as it is recognized that the system is a relative one and that the numbers carry no inherent, absolute meaning, the system can be used. A 100-point scale is acceptable to most people and one they feel they can interpret. If we can assure that this interpretation is not as a percent and so long as we do not attach too much significance to minor differences, the scale can be profitably employed.

The letter system. The type of grade most frequently encountered in contemporary schools is the letter grade. The letters most often used are A, B, C, D, and F. Sometimes E is used in place of F. The letters are frequently defined by such words as "excellent" or "superior" for A, "good" or "above average" for B, "satisfactory" or "average" for C, "poor" or "below average" for D, and "unsatisfactory" or "failing" for F. It will be noted that this is basically a five-point rating scale. It will also be noted that the meaning of the points on this scale is not very specific and that the words used to define the letters do little to improve the situation.

Most teachers would concede that the letter system was an improvement over the percentage system. It more clearly recognizes the relative nature of the assessment of achievement, and it avoids the necessity of making as many fine distinctions in that achievement. Also, it is more easily adapted to the evaluation of achievement in the light of ability. If the C grade is thought of as meaning "satisfactory" it is logical to assign this grade to the student of lower ability who is achieving as well as can be expected. The D grade is then reserved for the student who is judged to be capable of improvement if he works more diligently, and the F for those whose work is definitely "unsatisfactory." When this modification is used, and it is used widely, it should be recognized that, at least at the lower end of the scale, the grade is basically dependent on effort.

Many teachers feel that five degrees of achievement is an inadequate number. They, therefore, augment the scale by the use of plus and minus with the letter. The criticism is generally most severe with regard to the middle range of C grade. As the system is generally employed, more grades of C are assigned than of any other grade. Consequently, the range of achievement indicated by this grade may be considerable. Teachers are frequently disturbed by the fact that the near-B student is considerably superior to the near-D student, but both receive the same grade. Obviously, this is one of the major weaknesses of the system. A scale with more categories, perhaps a numerical scale, might be an improvement.

Numerical scales. With the increasingly wider use of data processing equipment by school systems, it has become apparent that a numerical grading scale may be more convenient than a letter scale. Computers manipulate with numbers rather than letters. When we calculate grade point averages from letter grades, we first have to convert them into numbers, so why not start with numbers?

A wide choice of numerical scales is, of course, possible. The simplest approach is to convert the letter grade into a numerical one. Usually this is done by assigning a 4 to the grade of A, a 3 to B, and so forth down to a 0 for the F. To provide for more categories, a decimal place may be added so that the scale would extend from 4.0 at the top to 0.0 at the bottom. This scale has long been used by the armed forces. For computer processing it has the slight disadvantage of requiring two columns on the data card. The stanine system of standard scores could easily be adapted to grading purposes. It offers more categories than the five-point letter scale but requires only one column on a data card.

A possible limitation of numerical scales may arise from the general tendency to interpret them as indicating relative position within a single group. If it is felt that individual achievement should be judged in relation to students of similar ability, a number scale may be even more susceptible to misinterpretation than a letter scale.

Graphic rating scales. Many schools, particularly elementary schools, prefer not to use specific grades. The reason most frequently advanced is that there are too many emotional connotations attached to such grades. A student can be "branded" by the type of grades he receives. Consequently, a system using somewhat more indefinite symbolism is preferred.

Generally, such schools employ some form of graphic rating scale when reporting student achievement to parents. This may be a simple scale using words such as superior, above average, average, below average, and unsatisfactory to indicate achievement levels, or they may be the more complex descriptive graphic scale that gives a brief characterization of the nature of the achievement at each level for each item reported.

There may be some question whether the use of such rating scales achieves the intended purpose. Most parents have been rather well conditioned to think in terms of letter grades, and they are likely to turn descriptive categories into such grades no matter how well intentioned school personnel may be in avoiding them.

Dichotomous scales. Within the past few years it has become fashionable to adopt a dichotomous rather than a five-point marking scale. Generally, the two categories are labeled *pass-fail* or *satisfactory-unsatisfactory*. Such scales have typically been adopted as a result of pressure from students. The usual argument in their favor is an educational one. Students claim that a pass-fail system relieves some of the pressures that inevitably accompany letter grading. Particularly in subjects one is taking merely to extend his area of general knowledge and competence, one should not have to worry about working for grades. A simple "pass" is sufficient to demonstrate reasonable effort and achievement.

One criticism which can be leveled at a dichotomous system is that it will be less reliable than one with five points. Similarly, a five-point scale will be less reliable than a ten-point scale. This reduction in reliability is statistical in nature and related to the truncated scale. If attention on a five- or ten-point scale is concentrated only on those who pass and those who fail, the difference in reliability may not exist. However, when a pass-fail system is adopted, teachers too frequently assume that the evaluation of achievement is simplified, that the pass-fail decision is an easy one to make. Quite often it is assumed that testing and other systematic attempts to measure achievement are no longer necessary. When this is the case the pass-fail judgment is highly subjective and based upon casual observation, and such judgments are highly susceptible to error. Under these conditions the reliability of the judgments can be seriously questioned. It should be noted that these judgments are at the most crucial point on the scale. The student who receives a C when he should have received a B has probably suffered no irreparable harm. The student who receives a Fail when he should have received a Pass will probably not view the situation so charitably. Certainly the pass-fail judgment should be based on the most valid assessment of achievement that can be devised.

The dichotomous scale has been suggested as especially appropriate to the evaluation of achievement in terms of student ability. The recommended dichotomy is usually "satisfactory-unsatisfactory." If the work of a bright student is no better than that of the median student, it may be judged unsatisfactory for him. The work of the slow learner may be accepted as satisfactory even though it may be the poorest in the class. In operation this system has encountered some difficulty from two sources. First, teachers are frequently dissatisfied with only two levels in the system. Often a third grade, "needs to improve" is introduced as descriptive of some pupils whose work is not so poor as to be "unsatisfactory." Second, while most teachers find no difficulty in judging the work of a slow learner satisfactory when they feel it demonstrates the student's best effort, they find it more difficult to judge the work of the bright student unsatisfactory when it is as good or better than that of most of the other students. With these two tendencies operating together the system has been known to end with grades of S+, S, S-, N, and U and to be indistinguishable from the more conventional letter grades.

DETERMINING GRADES

If grading is one of the most onerous tasks the teacher faces, determining which students should receive which grades is one of the most perplexing tasks. It is safe to say that neither teachers nor students are ever fully satisfied that complete justice has been done when grades are determined. There will always be the student who fell "one point short of a B" who believes the teacher has deliberately sabotaged his academic career. We are not so bold as to believe what we say in this section will do much to change this situation. What we would like to do is to show how some teachers *do* assign grades and discuss the pros and cons of these procedures.

Methods of determining grades. Undoubtedly the most talked about method of determining grades is *grading on the curve*. Fortunately for most students, the method is more talked about than employed. Furthermore, when people do talk about grading on the curve, they misuse the expression.

Strictly speaking, "grading on the curve" refers to the practice of assigning fixed percentages of grades to every class. The exact percentages may differ from teacher to teacher, but one traditional apportionment is 7 percent A's, 23 percent B's, 40 percent C's, 23 percent D's, and 7 percent F's. Note that this apportionment is symmetrical, that is, the percentage of A's is equal to the percentage of F's and the percentage of B's is equal to the percentage of D's. The symmetry of apportionment was justified, theoretically, on the basis that achievement was a normally distributed, continuous variable; thus, grades should reflect this distribution.

Actually, there are very few teachers who grade on the curve in the sense that they assign fixed and symmetrical distributions of grades. All teachers engage in some form of relative grading, but their grades are seldom symmetrically distributed. Most teachers are aware, implicitly if not explicitly, that the assumption of a normal distribution of achievement for their classes is unwarranted. Particularly, the lowest levels of achievement are not to be found in the typical class. An inspection of the grades teachers actually assign will always show more A's than F's.

Another method for determining grades from test scores is one which employs the standard deviation to establish cutting points. The presumed advantage of this system is that it needs no assumption of normality of distribution to justify its use.

A typical system is one which defines the five letter grades as follows:

A—Any score +1.5 σ or higher
B—Any score between +.5 and +1.5 σ
C—Any score between -.5 and +.5 σ
D—Any score between -1.5 and -.5 σ
F—Any score -1.5 σ or lower

When this system of converting test scores into grades was first introduced, its proponents claimed that it was better than grading on the curve because it took the shape of the distribution into account. That is, if a distribution of scores was markedly positively skewed, conceivably there might not be any grades of F assigned because no score would fall lower than -1.5 σ. Conversely, in a negatively skewed distribution, there might not be any A's. Most teachers now recognize, however, that the shape of the distribution of test scores is, to a large extent, a function of the difficulty level of the items in that test. We can produce positively skewed distributions by using only difficult items, and we can produce negatively skewed distributions by using only easy items. Since the distribution of test scores is more a function of item difficulty than of the basic achievement of the group tested, it is difficult to justify this method of determining grades as any real improvement over grading on the curve.

Undoubtedly the system of converting test scores to grades used by the majority of teachers is the *inspection* method. In this method, the teacher constructs a frequency distribution of scores; then he usually inspects this distribution to choose likely cutting points for grades. Sometimes he looks for *breaks* in the distribution and selects his cutting points at these score values where no frequency occurs.

This method of determining grades is undoubtedly an improvement over the two methods just described, but it does have at least two weaknesses. First, breaks in a distribution are largely a matter of chance. A teacher depending upon the existence of such breaks to provide him with cutting points may grade somewhat erratically. Second, erratic grading results in inequities to students. The same score on the same test may receive a B one term and a C the next term.

Perhaps the most defensible system of grading is to establish certain broad ranges of percentages of the class to which certain grades may be assigned. For example, one such system might look like this:

A—10-20 percent
B—15-30 percent
C—40-60 percent
D—10-20 percent
F— 0-10 percent

This approach to grading possesses certain advantages. First, it provides for a certain degree of uniformity from term to term by a single teacher. Second, if accepted by a number of teachers in the same area, it provides for a degree of uniformity among teachers, perhaps an even more serious defect in the way grades are usually assigned. Third, it allows for differences in grades based upon differences in class ability level. This matter will be discussed in greater detail in the next section.

Factors to take into account in converting scores to grades. Teachers are aware that grades cannot always be uniformly assigned for one class to another or for one term to another. The major factor which militates against such uniformity is the factor of ability. Some classes are simply more able than others. So far as grading is concerned, the question is whether more able classes should receive higher grades.

The obvious answer to this question is that yes, ability level should be a factor in determining grades. To eliminate it would be an obvious hardship for the higher ability student.

There are certain types of classes where ability level may be a special problem. Most obviously these would be accelerated or honors classes and retarded or remedial classes. Certainly it seems justified to claim that most honors students should receive either A or B if they do the work required of them. It seems somewhat less palatable, to claim by the same logic, that remedial students should receive either F or D. In either case, however, there should be nothing to prevent any particular student from receiving a C if the caliber of his work merits the grade.

Sometimes a teacher has no particular reason to believe that one class is more able than another. He simply "feels" this is the case. It is always possible to check the veracity of this feeling by referring to measures of academic ability found in the usual school record system. If the "feeling" does not result in large deviations from customary practice, however, it is probably reasonably safe for the teacher to indulge his whims, knowing he probably has not done incalculable harm to any given student.

Composite measures in grading. When it comes to assigning final grades, a teacher frequently wishes to combine a number of measures into a composite of some sort. The individual measures themselves should always be retained in the teacher's records in their original forms, that is, as raw scores rather than grades. Too much information will be lost if the measures are converted to grades and then combined to form a composite grade. Consequently, we shall discuss how to combine raw scores into a composite measure.

The general principle which governs such combinations is that the weight a given measure brings to a composite is a function of two things: (1) the variability of that measure, and (2) its correlation with the other measures. In general classroom practice, it is difficult or impractical to determine the latter, so we restrict ourselves to the former. The standard deviation provides us with our best measure of variability for combining measures.

The precise techniques for combining measures have been more thoroughly discussed in Chapter 9 under the heading of standard scores. By converting raw scores to standard scores, we can assign weights to the several measures enabling us to produce a composite score accurately reflecting the importance assigned to each of the measures. Of the several types of standard scores that will perform this service, the stanine is probably easiest for the teacher to understand and employ.

Appendix
DERIVATION
OF
FORMULA (2.3)

$$G$$iven two scores (S_1 and S_2) for each of N individuals, the coefficient of correlation between the scores (r_{12}) is given by

$$r_{12} = \frac{\Sigma s_1 s_2}{N\sigma_1 \sigma_2},$$

(A.1)

where s_1 and s_2 are the scores expressed as deviations from their respective means ($s = S - \overline{S}$), and σ_1 and σ_2 are the respective standard deviations.

It follows that

$$\Sigma s_1 s_2 = r_{12} N\sigma_1 \sigma_2,$$

(A.2)

and it should be noted that if the scores are statistically independent (uncorrelated), r_{12} will equal zero and $\Sigma s_1 s_2$ will also equal zero.

Let

$$S = T + E + \text{E}, \tag{A.3}$$

where T is the true score, E is the score for lasting and systematic errors of measurement, and E is the score for temporary and/or chance errors. (By definition T, E, and E are statistically independent.)

Then

$$\bar{S} = \bar{T} + \bar{E} + \bar{\text{E}}$$
$$s = S - \bar{S} = (T - \bar{T}) + (E - \bar{E}) + (\text{E} - \bar{\text{E}})$$
$$= t + e + \epsilon,$$
$$s^2 = t^2 + e^2 + \epsilon^2 + 2te + 2t\epsilon + 2e\epsilon,$$
$$\Sigma s^2 = \Sigma t^2 + \Sigma e^2 + \Sigma \epsilon^2 \tag{A.4}$$

since the sums of the cross-products of independent variables equal zero [see (A.2) above].

It follows that

$$\sigma_S^2 = \sigma_t^2 + \sigma_e^2 + \sigma_\epsilon^2. \tag{A.5}$$

The total variance of a set of scores is, thus, the sum of the variances of the true scores, the lasting and systematic errors, and the temporary and/or chance errors.

The validity of a test is the degree to which the test measures consistently the characteristic(s) it is used to measure. The coefficient of validity (r_v) is the correlation coefficient between the test scores (S) and a perfectly reliable criterion (C). Since the criterion is a theoretically perfect measure of the true score,

$$c = t,$$

and from (A.5),

$$\sigma_c^2 = \sigma_t^2.$$

Also,

$$sc = (t + e + \epsilon)t = t^2 + te + t\epsilon,$$
$$\Sigma sc = \Sigma t^2,$$

the other terms again vanishing.

$$\frac{\Sigma sc}{N} = \sigma_t^2,$$

therefore,

$$r_v = \frac{\sigma_t^2}{\sigma_s \sigma_c} = \frac{\sigma_t^2}{\sigma_t \sqrt{\sigma_t^2 + \sigma_e^2 + \sigma_\epsilon^2}} = \frac{\sigma_t}{\sqrt{\sigma_t^2 + \sigma_e^2 + \sigma_\epsilon^2}} \qquad (A.6)$$

$$r_v^2 = \frac{\sigma_t^2}{\sigma_t^2 + \sigma_e^2 + \sigma_\epsilon^2}.$$

The square of the validity coefficient is, thus, the proportion of the total variance of the test scores that is attributable to the variance in true scores.

The relevance of a test is the degree to which the lasting and systematic factors that the test measures agree with those the test is used to measure. The coefficient of relevance ($r_{..}$) is the correlation coefficient between a perfectly reliable test score ($S = T + E$) and a perfectly reliable criterion ($C = T$). In a proof similar to that for r_v, it can be shown that

$$r_{..}^2 = \frac{\sigma_t^2}{\sigma_t^2 + \sigma_e^2}. \qquad (A.7)$$

The square of the coefficient of relevance is the proportion of the lasting and systematic variance which is variance in true scores.

The reliability of a test is the consistency with which the test measures whatever it does measure. The reliability coefficient (r_{xx}) is obtained from the correlation between two scores from the same test for each of the members of the same group. Now, if S_1 and S_2 represent these two scores,

$$s_1 = t + e + E_1 \quad \text{and} \quad s_2 = t + e + \epsilon_2,$$

where ϵ_1 and ϵ_2 are the deviation scores for temporary and/or chance errors differentially affecting the two scores. These error scores are, of course, independent of each other as well as of t and e.

Now,

$$s_1 s_2 = t^2 + e^2 + 2te + t\epsilon_1 + t\epsilon_2 + e\epsilon_1 + e\epsilon_2 + \epsilon_1 \epsilon_2,$$
$$\Sigma s_1 s_2 = \Sigma t^2 + \Sigma e^2,$$

the sums of the other terms again vanishing, and

$$\frac{\Sigma s_1 s_2}{N} = \sigma_t^2 + \sigma_e^2.$$

The reliability coefficient is then

$$r_{xx} = \frac{\sigma_t^2 + \sigma_e^2}{\sigma s_1 \sigma s_2}. \tag{A.8}$$

Now, if S_1 and S_2 are measures from the same test, any difference between the standard deviations should be due to chance, and we may assume that $\sigma s_1 \sigma s_2$ is an estimate of σ_s^2, the total variance of the scores. Applying (A.5), formula (A.8) becomes

$$r_{xx} = \frac{\sigma_t^2 + \sigma_e^2}{\sigma_t^2 + \sigma_e^2 + \sigma_\epsilon^2}. \tag{A.9}$$

The reliability coefficient itself (rather than its square) is the proportion of the total variance that can be attributed to lasting and systematic factors.

Now, formula (A.6) may be written:

$$r_v^2 = \left(\frac{\sigma_t^2}{\sigma_t^2 + \sigma_e^2 + \sigma_\epsilon^2} \right) \left(\frac{\sigma_t^2 + \sigma_e^2}{\sigma_t^2 + \sigma_e^2} \right) = \left(\frac{\sigma_t^2}{\sigma_t^2 + \sigma_e^2} \right) \left(\frac{\sigma_t^2 + \sigma_e^2}{\sigma_t^2 + \sigma_e^2 + \sigma_\epsilon^2} \right).$$

Applying Formulas (A.7) and (A.8), we have

$$r_v^2 = r_{..}^2 \, r_{xx} \tag{A.10}$$

and

$$r_v = r_{..} \sqrt{r_{xx}} \tag{A.11}$$

Formula (A.11) is the same as Formula (2.3).

INDEX

absolute system of grading, 140, 195
academic achievement, 13
alternate response items, 74
anecdotal records, 47–50
arithmetic mean, *see* mean
averages, *see* central tendency

bar graphs, 152–154
Bloom, B. S., 39–40, 98
blueprint, *see* table of specifications
Buros, O. K., 142

central tendency, 156
    mean, 161–167
    median, 158–161
    mode, 157–158
chance, guessing in test iems, 22
    influence on test scores, 21, 23
    in the selection of test iems, 22
check lists, 50–51
classification items, 97–99
coefficient of correlation, 14
completion items, *see* short-answer item form
confidence weighting, 76–77
continuous variables, 3
correction for guessing, 116–117
criterion-referenced tests, 41–42
criterion scores, 18
Cureton, E. E., 27

descriptive statistics, 146–147
deviation scores, 163–164
diagnostic tests, 140–141
difficulty, *see* item difficulty
discontinuous variable, 3
discrimination, *see* item discrimination
distractors, 81

educational achievement, 8, 23

educational objectives, 32–33
    behavioral definitions of, 34
    formulation of, 35–41
empirical relevance, 18
equivalent forms reliability, 14–16
equivalent test forms, 13–14
error of measurement, 11–12, 20, 23–30
essay items, 99–108
exercise, test, 94

frequency distributions, 147–152
frequency polygons, 152, 154–156

grading, 186–189
    absolute, 140, 195
    on the curve, 200–201
    pass-fail, 198–200

halo effect, 64, 108
histograms, 152–154

interval limits, 154
interval scale, 5
item analysis, 118–120
item difficulty, 121–125
item discrimination, 126–129
item editing, 110
item files, 135–137
item forms, 69–70
    classification, 97–99
    essay, 99–108
    matching, 94–97
    multiple-choice, 81–94
    short-answer, 70–73
    true-false, 73–81
item revision, 132–134
item weighting, 117

Kuder-Richardson formula, 17

Mager, R. E., 37–38

76 77 78 79 80   10 9 8 7 6 5 4